Reader

I have known Dr. Massey for a number of years. During that time, he had quietly and consistently completed an amazing number of incredible humanitarian projects while conducting a very successful professional life. While serving as the school superintendent of the largest K-8 public school system in California, I asked him how he found the time and resources to help so many of the children in my district. Mind Realignment – Naked Secrets for Building a Better You is his answer to my question. It is a remarkable collection of thought and advice intended to unleash the power within you. I have met many people who enrich the world through serving their fellow man. But very few have succeeded in accomplishing the goals that they set for themselves and almost no one sets the bar as high as Dr. Massey. I urge you to read this book. I will be applying its message chapter by chapter, day by day to my own life and work. Dr. Massey is a tough act to follow, but he has left a trail for us to take, if we will only aspire to making the world a better place.

The Honorable Jean Fuller, PhD.
State of California Assembly Member, 32nd District

If you are looking for practical wisdom, incisive insight, hearty encouragement and wisdom both current and past, look no further! Drawing widely from many sources as well as using his own pen, Manzoor Massey has provided us all with what we much need—wisdom for life. This book will, no doubt, bless and inspire and challenge and change you.

Randall L. Roberts, Senior Pastor
Loma Linda University, Loma Linda, California

Practical, simple, but provocative tool to realign the minds of all who are willing to part with their unproductive past and experience a more rewarding future. Dr. Massey was vice-president of my corporation. I requested him to apply the wisdom of his book to train my executive teams. If heeded, this book will build better families, better communities and better businesses.

Jose Arredondo, Businessman
Bakersfield, California

Dr. Massey has written an empowering, uplifting, and inspiring book for us all. Through his many years of experience and study, he has compiled a wealth of valuable wisdom, and he has graciously passed them on to us. I wholeheartedly recommend that you read this book with an open heart and mind and get ready for real "nuggets" of truth that apply to real life, and can be transformational!

Pastor James Ranger
Bakersfield New Life Center

Dr. Massey is a keen student of human behavior and its impact on life. In Mind Realignment for Excellence he presents succinct and practical advice for rebuilding your life. Best of all, it illustrates and advocates balance – the very quality that is so easily lost in the juggling of competing priorities that form our daily agendas. The book's format is best suited for the "baby-boomer - iPod generation."

Lowell C. Cooper, General Vice President
General Conference of Seventh-day Adventists. Washington D. C.

Dr. Massey's "Mind Realignment – Naked Secrets for Building a Better You" is to the serious person what the power-bar is to the devoted athlete. It is full of succinct and powerful statements packed with energy. All it takes to fall upon a pearl of wisdom is to just open a page and look anywhere and it lands on the bull's eye each time. The reflection given to digest it, and the effort spent in applying it, is bound to be rewarded with lasting inner healing.

Devadas Moses, MD, DrPH.
Loma Linda, Californi

Mind Realignment for Excellence

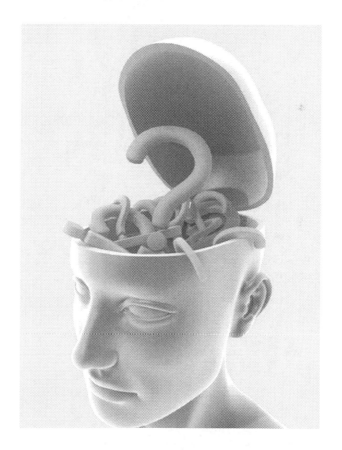

Naked Secrets for Building a Better You

Volume II

Manzoor R. Massey, Ph.D., M.P.H.

Order this book online at www.trafford.com
or email orders@trafford.com

Most Trafford titles are also available at major online book retailers.

ISBN: 978-1-4269-3262-5 (sc)
ISBN: 978-1-4269-3263-2 (hc)
ISBN: 978-1-4269-3264-9 (eBook)

Library of Congress Control Number: 2010906833

Our mission is to efficiently provide the world's finest, most comprehensive book publishing
service, enabling every author to experience success. To find out how to publish your book,
your way, and have it available worldwide, visit us online at www.trafford.com

Trafford rev. 7/30/2010

 www.trafford.com

North America & international
toll-free: 1 888 232 4444 (USA & Canada)
phone: 250 383 6864 ♦ fax: 812 355 4082

Naked Secrets for Building a Better You

Table of Contents

MYTHS ABOUT MOTIVATION

IMPROVE YOURSELF TO IMPROVE THE WORLD

TREAT YOUR BODY BETTER THAN YOUR CAR

JOURNEY WITH JOY

INVEST IN THE SOIL OF YOUR SOUL

WHEN ALL IS SAID AND DONE

Foreword

TO COMMEND THE work of a friend of long standing always gives one pleasure; when that friend is one's former student, the satisfaction is multiplied. Manzoor Massey was my student when I taught at Spicer Memorial College in Pune, India, many years ago.

Although "Mind Realignment for Excellence" isn't written as biography, it, in fact, flows out of the life of Dr. Manzoor Massey. It reflects the convictions and passions that have made him what he is and enabled him to become a prominent health-care professional and a very creative and dynamic communicator.

This is a valuable book. For everyone who seeks to develop their God-given potential, it is a strong motivator. For everyone who is ready to grow up and quit whining, who is tired of blaming family or fate for their lot in life, this book can provide practical suggestions and incentives to break clean from the past and to start living in the power of their individuality.

Manzoor Massey is a high-energy, creative, positive individual who loves life and its challenges. And I applaud his efforts to share with others the secrets of his success. This book can turn lives around for the better. I wish "Mind Realignment for Excellence" every success.

William G. Johnsson. Ph.D., D. D.
Silver Spring, Maryland

Acknowledgments

I OWE SPECIAL gratitude to my father who, very early in my life, taught me the art of realigning my mind. He taught me that one positive example is worth more than a million words of good advice. Right from the start my father engraved on my mind, "Don't ask anyone to do anything that you are unwilling to do if you have the skill or the time. Work with your heart and not just with your mind. Remember, wisdom is more desirable than knowledge, and vision is more important than 20/20 eyesight." I wish today that I had listened to him with more passion when he was laying the foundation and sculpting my life.

I am grateful to my loving wife who patiently inspired me to adhere to the principles of commonsense in writing this book. She taught me that when all is said and done, position, power, popularity and privileges all fade away. So I had better focus on the art of building people and relationships, for that is the real secret of building a better you. Build people, help them achieve their goals and watch them stun you by unleashing their unlimited potential to enhance your life and future. By building people, you can climb any mountain, cross any ocean, survive any desert storm, find your way through a dense fog, see a rainbow while drenched in the pouring rain, and sing when you have every reason to weep.

I am grateful to my children, Myron and Mistina, who continuously teach me that I cannot go forward in reverse gear because there is no future in the past. My children are great snowboarders. Their adventurous spirit has taught me that whatever the mind can conceive, the body can deliver. If more coaches saw the finish line, more teams would score their goals.

Special thanks go to a visionary leader, Jose Arredondo, who founded 12 successful companies in nine years. It was my privilege to work as his vice president and test the principles described in this book. My deep gratitude to Eloise Mattison for her editorial skills. Without her able assistance, this work could not have been completed. I want to thank Pastor W. Gordon Jenson, who patiently reviewed various drafts and made many valuable suggestions to improve this book. Special thanks to my friends Bernice and Barry Lowenstein for their careful review and recommendations. Finally, my special gratitude to Dr. William G. Johnsson, one of my mentors whose life and leadership inspired me to write this book.

This book contains many mind realignment secrets. If taken seriously, its contents will build better people, better families, better neighborhoods, better cities, better states, better nations, and make the world a better place to live, work and build more purposeful lives. The naked secrets presented in this book elude the most sophisticated mind! By the fact that you are reading this, you are already a cut above the ordinary person. I dedicate this book to you. May it provide you many practical ideas to build a better you and add value to everything and everyone you touch!

A Word to the Reader

THIS BOOK IS written for busy people like you who eat on-the-run and live in the fast lane. The lifestyle of many these days is – go, go, get an ulcer and if you can get one today, why wait for tomorrow? Knowing that no one enjoys reading long-winded boring discourses, each chapter is kept short. Each chapter is written to provide you a unique and practical thought to share with your family, friends and co-workers. It is hoped that the reading of this book will make a profound effect in the way you think, believe and behave.

I was editing this book on a plane, when an inquisitive neighbor saw the title and remarked, "Mind Realignment -- Naked Secrets of Building a Better You! What a strange title for a book. How could it be a secret if it is naked?" she asked. "Wisdom is obvious. It weeps bitterly, begging us to allow it to guide us on our journey of life, and yet we do not recognize it. We ignore it, thinking it is just a ghost from the past, pestering us to listen to its fables," I replied. "How true!" said the lady. Let me share with you a brief story to emphasize an important principle that may help you get more from reading this book.

Two attorneys wanted to explore the world. "Let's not do the same thing others do," said one of them. "What do you have in mind?" inquired the other. "Let's ride in a balloon instead of a plane or a boat." So they got into a balloon. They had barely lifted up when the wind got stronger, clouds got thicker and they began to drift towards the ocean. In panic, one of them shouted, "We don't even know where we are. No one will know our whereabouts if we crash." Just then they spotted a fellow walking on the beach. They looked down and shouted, "Hi there, where are we?" The man on the beach responded, "You are in a balloon." That started an argument between the two attorneys. "That man is also an attorney," said one of them. "How can you be so sure," asked the other. "I can bet my bottom dollar that the man on the beach is also an attorney." "But how can you be so sure," inquired his friend. "Well, the information he has provided is precisely accurate but utterly useless."

The mind realignment secrets in this book are based on age-old proven wisdom, and they meet the test of "commonsense." These secrets are based on personal experiences, a lifetime of observations and listening to wise gurus who have crossed my path. However, they will not be worth a hill of beans unless you take them to heart. Don't be cynical because they seem to be too simple. Remember, a simple amateur carpenter built Noah's Ark, while learned engineers built the Titanic. Don't look for complicated and sophisticated theories. When it comes to building a better you, one simple and practical idea you can use is worth more than 1000 fancy plans safely tucked away in a golden box in your treasure chest. Read it, share it, and make a difference in your world!

Writing this book was an adventure. At first I intended to write only the first Volume. However, the more I explored my mind, the more treasures I discovered, and more eager I was to share with my readers. There is no limit to what we can learn, if we only keep our mouth shut and mind open. Those who proofed the first volume encouraged me to write volume II. Although each volume is complete in itself, the second volume would propel the reader's mind to a new height and a greater depth of self-actualization and growth.

Manzoor R. Massey, Ph.D., M.P.H., Author

Conquer Greed
–It's Nothing More
Than a Bad Weed

WHEN I WAS a child, my father often told me stories to teach me important principles of life. To teach me the consequences of being greedy, he shared with me a story that I want to pass on to you. Think about it and take it to heart. It will change your life.

There lived a man by the name of Ali Hafiz. His parents died and left him a lot of money. He bought 80 camels and began a transportation business. One day he met a Holy Man who advised him to follow him and he would show him great treasures in a mountain cave. However, he wanted Ali Hafiz to promise that when the camels are loaded with treasures, he would give twenty camels to the Holy Man and keep 60 for himself. Ali Hafiz agreed and the journey began.

When they arrived at the foot of the mountain, the Holy Man asked Ali to see the mountain through a small little box with his left eye. He further advised him that if Ali insisted on seeing the mountain through his right eye, he would go blind. Ali saw the mountain with his left eye and was amazed to see the hidden treasures. He loaded up 80 camels and agreed to hand over 20 camels to the Holy Man.

After a few miles, Ali approached the Holy Man and told him that it was a lot of work to take care of 20 camels. Perhaps he should keep only 15 so he would not be distracted from his spiritual activities. The Holy Man agreed. A little later, Ali approached him again and emphasized the amount of time it would take to feed 15 camels. Perhaps the Holy Man should keep only ten, said Ali. The man agreed. Finally, Ali approached him again and pleaded for the man to concentrate on his spiritual mission instead of worrying about the camels. The Holy Man agreed and gave Ali all the camels and went on his way. They had hardly gone fifty yards when Ali ran after the man and asked for the little box so in case he runs out of the treasures, he would be able to go back to the mountain. The Holy Man tried his best to persuade Ali against using the box but to no avail. Finally, he received the box and thought, "If I could see so many treasures with my left eye, the man must be cheating me by prohibiting me to see with my right eye." He looked through the box with his right eye and instantly went blind. Soon someone stole his camels.

As Ali sat in front of a holy shrine begging for alms, he would ask people to also hit him at the back of his head to remind him that he was not only poor but also a greedy fool. One can become greedy for money, more credit than deserved or a house one cannot afford. I have encountered many who could have gained much had they remained open to contentment instead of greed.

SOMETHING TO THINK ABOUT

Greed is a cancer. It robs people of peace of mind. Think of ways you can conquer greed.

The Dream Seekers and the Dream Robbers

THE YEAR 2008 stripped America's passion for being rich and drove her to poverty many had not seen for nearly seventy-five years. The beginning of the 21st Century in America was marked with euphoria and intense depression. We saw the demise of a giant Enron that plunged thousands of businesses into deep despair, beyond repair. We saw its chief commit suicide after being assured of a long prison term. We saw another towering business empire, Arthur Anderson, a company that specialized in accounting and auditing go down the tube in disgrace for cooking books for greedy and dishonest corporations. Then we saw the government getting preoccupied with war in Iraq and neglecting the domestic affairs. As the old saying goes, "When the cat is away, the mice will play." While the government looked elsewhere, the greedy banks and financial institutions doled out money to people who, in reality could not qualify to purchase a toaster. With nothing down, and no evidence, or shoddy evidence, people could realize the "American Dream" of owning a house. Millions of homes were built in 2005-2007.

Then came 2008 when economic reality hit the global markets. The two giant companies, Freddie Mac and Fannie Mae that held more than 50% of all the mortgages in America went belly up. We saw oil prices go to five dollars a gallon. Was there a real reason? Yes! Greed and lack of conscience on the part of the oil companies and the snoring champions of deregulation. Truckers felt the pinch! They could not make a living while paying over five dollars a gallon for diesel. Families had to choose between paying for gasoline or for medicine for their aged family members. Many, drowning in debt, worked on two or three part-time jobs to make ends meet while neglecting their families and children. However, the politicians kept on trucking in their gas-guzzlers. No one paid attention until the Stock Market and Wall Street were about to breathe their last; then all eyes popped out. Although public speeches paid lip service to save the "hard-working families," the real reason for the bailout was to save the fat cats who had a lot to lose if their investments in the Stock Market and the housing and banking industries went down the chute. The housing values fell to an all-time low. The price of our residence went down by $200,000.

It was the year of the Presidential election in America. Senators Barack Obama and John McCain were the two presidential candidates. They accused each other of falling asleep at the wheel while being part of the Washington establishment. Both believed they had the medicine to save the dying American economic machine. On September 22, 2008, President George W. Bush came up with a grand plan to mortgage the future of the working American families by doling out $700 billion to save Wall Street, the giant banks, their investors and shareholders. While the poor home-owners were struggling to pay their mortgages and facing foreclosures, the ones who made greedy choices and killed the economy were being rescued. CEO's of the failed corporations were retiring with astronomical perks and parachutes.

Congress was holding hearings to gift the $700 billion on behalf of the taxpayers to those who profited from the run-away housing boom in 2007. Lawmakers were feverishly working to rescue their friends in the banking world while wearing ear-mufflers to shut off the cry of the poor taxpayers who had to foot the bill. While lying on its own economic death bed, America was spending $10 billion a month on the war in Iraq, the country that had a $79 billion surplus. Sanity had been awarded a one-way ticket to another world and banished from the American soil. We had entered an era of "Survival of the Fittest." I am an optimist. I believe that just like after the depression of 1930's, America will survive and prosper again. I am also a realist. I strongly believe that after the effects of the economic hurricane or tsunami are past, selfishness, greed, dishonesty, shady financial practices will again reign in the American corporate board rooms. The unscrupulous policies of Wall Street and the banking industry will again raise their ugly heads and the innocent American will be preyed upon in the name of progress.

Two classes of Americans will rise again: the "Dream Seekers" and the "Dream Robbers." I salute the "Dream Seekers." These are the optimists, hardworking, tax-paying, flag-saluting and patriotic Americans. They will try to capture every opportunity they can to build a better future for their families. The "Dream Seekers" will be active participants in the life of their schools, their churches, their neighborhoods, their communities and their nation. They will attempt to bring pride and honor back to America again. However, it seems that the "Dream Seekers" can never match the trickery and skills of the "Dream Robbers." The "Dream Robbers" seem to be always a step ahead of the "Dream Seekers."

Misuse of the American system seems to be designed to help the "Dream Robbers" thrive while the "Dream Seekers" barely survive. The "Dream Robbers" will again run the banks, the housing industry, hog the corporate board rooms, manipulate Wall Street, and enact public policies that would reward the unscrupulous at the expense of the unknowing, hardworking, innocent "Dream Seekers." The American free market philosophy is based on the "Trust" factor. We reward those who have and trust that they will benefit those who are seeking the American dream. Absent from our basic premise is the "greed" factor. The trust factor is the ideal premise when human conscience is alive and well. Trust factor is a prescription for disaster when the conscience is dead and selfishness is on the throne. While I don't imply that everyone running the economic machine is conscience-challenged, without adequate public policies and oversight, the temptation takes the toll even of the best intentioned.

Dare I predict also that the average American will forget what we are going through! People will again borrow what they would not be able to pay back; make promises they have no intentions to keep; get into unproductive business dealings with hopes to make quick cash; spend more than they make; carry credit cards that they are not qualified to receive, and live hand-to-mouth. Dare I say that many Americans again will live fiscally irresponsible lives as though there was no day of reckoning? Many will remain just two paychecks away from bankruptcy.

What America, and for that matter the entire world, is going through is raising eyebrows around the globe. We are one big village now. What happens in one place sends shockwaves or good vibes to all corners of the world. In some respects, our actions and our destiny are becoming more and more interdependent. This phenomenon has made me acutely aware that my thoughts and actions have a profound influence on the lives of others around me. It goes like a ripple effect until everyone around the globe feels it. It means that I have to carefully realign my mind so my thoughts will build others, encourage them and ease their burdens. My business practices will be just, fair, legal as well as ethical.

SOMETHING TO THINK ABOUT

How would you realign your mind to ensure a better future for yourself and your family?

Know When Enough Is Enough

ONCE SOMEONE ASKED an oil magnet, who was one of world's richest men, as to how much more money a person in his shoes would need to feel successful. He replied, "Just a little bit more." During one summer when I was working for an international company selling books to earn my scholarship, I met a man with a large mansion – four cars parked in his driveway, and lots of children around the house. "You must be very happy," I said to the man. He looked at me and with a somber face replied, "Happiness and I have never been introduced to each other." I was so sorry to hear that. With obvious signs of all the material goods around him, I was certain he would be very happy with his blessings. I learned that he felt very poor and unsuccessful. He had lots of money but he lacked wealth, if you know what I mean!

When I was a student at a university in Michigan, I earned $34 a month. I paid $9 for my apartment, $4 I gave for charity, spent $9 on groceries and sent $12 to my brothers and sisters in India each month. I lived in an apartment complex known as the "Monastery" because five of us single men had a room each and we shared the bathroom, shower and the kitchen. All my bills were paid; I had no debt. I was happy and slept well at night. I had some rich classmates who lived in two-to-three bedroom apartments. They had cars, girlfriends, were popular but always broke and unhappy. By the middle of the month they were always puzzled why their money was over when the month was still half remaining. They were often heard calling parents for more money.

In America, my observation is that when people earn $10 they spend $15. When the expense goes to $15, they must try to earn $20. When they earn $20, the expense goes to $25. It seems that enough is never enough because we measure a person's worth not by what she/he has become but by what they have. You are building a better you; dare to be different!

No one has ever been able to satisfy a thirsty desert, hungry goat and an undisciplined human appetite. Volunteer at a homeless shelter to serve soup a few times and you will learn how little it really takes to experience real happiness and contentment.

SOMETHING TO THINK ABOUT

1. If you have a twelve-bedroom house, on how many beds can you sleep each night?

2. How much money would you take with you when you check out of this world?

3. How would you like to be remembered at the end of your journey?

4. If you have five cars, how many cars can you drive at a time?

5. What does "enough is enough" mean to you?

Don't Resort to Shortcuts

DON'T BE IN a hurry if you want to reach your destination safely. Just plan better and start early, earlier the better. On the journey of life, there are no shortcuts. In fact, when we take a shortcut, we often wind up taking a detour that leads to a dead-end. People who resort to shortcuts, often cut their life short. There is a natural process to get things done. Defying the process usually lands us in spending more time and working harder. Postponed thinking and lack of planning may force us to rush, but it is usually unproductive exercise. In the absence of hunger in our soul to get the best out of life, we often look for fast lanes to get us to our destinations. However, we wind up at unexpected and undesirable destinations.

Some people searching for peace of mind resort to Valium to forget their pain. Americans consume almost $550 million worth of Valium each year. Today, there are 700 different drugs resembling Valium alone. It equals 142 tablets of Valium for every man, woman and child in the United States per year (2000 estimates from the U.S. Food and Drug Administration). Someone has been taking my share as well because I have never had even one pill thus far. When the effects of Valium wear out, the person feels even worse. Popping a pill does not cure the problem, it just postpones one's thinking about it.

In an average American home, you will find pain pills strategically placed throughout the house, because people don't know where they might be when they develop a headache. A headache is a thermometer that tells us that the body is overtaxed and abused. It is not a green light to pop another pill. Instead of dealing with our problems and resolving them, we tend to either ignore them, try to forget them or bury them, only to dig them up later for future pain and suffering.

To get rich in a hurry, some people sell illegal substances, lie, cheat and delude others, finally winding up in a prison or in a poorhouse. Many resort to buying lottery tickets to get their hands on some cold cash. I have listened to numerous lottery winners interviewed on television and radios. Six months after winning, most of them are broke and miserable. The money did not fix the broken spirit and the poverty of their soul. Shortcuts often lead to dead-end roads. I know of people who married with hopes to land a fat bank balance; however, they ended up cutting their life short. There are no shortcuts to gaining knowledge, wealth or wisdom.

Then there are those who feast on the "get-thin-quick" schemes, promoted by the "get-rich-quick" gurus who peddle gadgets and thousands of untested and unproven products. Many people are willing to sacrifice their life and money on false promises in the hope to look good and feel better. Then there are those dreamers who want to be rich and live in a country house with a white picket fence. However, when you ask them if they have a plan to realize their dreams, they simply shrug their shoulders. If you meet someone looking for a shortcut to get to his/her destination, be certain that such a person is on his way to a fantasy island. A dream without a plan is a nightmare.

SOMETHING TO THINK ABOUT

Can you identify some detours and deadends in your life?

Don't Bite the Hand That Feeds You

DURING MY CAREER I have had the opportunity to interview hundreds of candidates for employment. One of my favorite questions to the candidates has been, "Tell me three things you like about the company where you currently work?" I found many candidates at a loss for words. By the time people think of changing jobs, they have usually fallen out of love with their current job. They have developed a string of reasons to convince themselves why it is not a good place to work. They either dislike the coworkers, the boss or the working conditions. During the course of the interview, some have been quite expressive of their negative sentiments towards their current job. They freely drill holes in the bottom of the boat in which they are traveling. People who criticize their current place of work or show dislike for their co-workers, I usually don't consider fit for my team. Your best foundation to build your future career is the skills and attitude you develop at your current job. Your dislike for your current employer and the company would raise a red flag for your potential employer.

The average American worker changes his place of work every three years. Many get bored and lose interest in what they do. As one's enthusiasm declines to come to work, so does the performance. Such workers do just enough to avoid termination. They become unhappy, and like termites, they begin to erode the good name of the company. They become a cancer and compromise the performance of their colleagues. Such employees become "Job hoppers." Seeking upward mobility in one's profession is a noble aspiration; however, to quit a job due to lack of interest in it usually renders a person useless regardless of the change of job or location. Employees who put the interest of the company above their own will not lose interest in their job.

The company that builds its employees and invests in their future has little to worry about when the market gets rough and competition gets stiff. The workers will ensure the survival of the company. Employees who develop loyalty toward the company will have little to worry about when there is a slump in business. Here are a few tips for workers who want job security.

- Don't drill holes in the bottom of the ship in which you are traveling. If the ship does not make it to the shore, you will be lost at sea.

- Don't wait to do your best to build the company until they pay you more. The employer rewards performance, not a promise.

- Don't tear down the company or your coworkers. If you weaken the company ship and it sinks, you will go down with it. Don't bite the hand that feeds you.

- Your credibility is directly in proportion to the reputation of your company. It makes sense to take pride in what you do and build the company that feeds your family.

- Remain loyal to your current employer – your next job depends on it.

SOMETHING TO THINK ABOUT

Write down ten things you can do to improve your performance on the job. Share with your supervisor three concrete suggestions to improve the company.

Be Faithful
Like Dorado

AFTER THE SEPTEMBER 11, 2001 event that shook the world, many stories appeared about the courage, patriotism, dedication and love for life displayed by people trying to rescue the victims of the most hateful crime against humanity. One of the most exciting stories I read was about the faithfulness of Dorado, friend of Omar Eduardo Rivera.

New York resident Omar Eduardo Rivera was stranded on the 71st floor of the World Trade Center north tower when the hijacked airliner struck the building 25 floors above him. Mr. Rivera, a computer specialist, was in his office with his friend Dorado beside him. The Contra Costa Times reported the miraculous rescue of Rivera by his friend Dorado. Mr. Rivera was blind. He knew that with thousands of people trying to escape the building, he would never be able to make it 71 floors down the stairs. He encouraged Dorado to leave him and save his own life. However, Dorado displayed the most exemplary unselfish love for his friend and did not leave. Dorado hung onto his friend Rivera and guided him down 71 flights of stairs through smoke-filled hallways, impatient people pushing and pulling, and all the noise of shattered glass and debris.

In the words of Eduardo Rivera, upon entering the street down from 71 floors, "It was then I knew for certain he loved me just as much as I loved him. He was prepared to die in the hope he might save my life...I owe my life to Dorado -- my companion and best friend" (reported in the Contra Costa Times, taken from The DogNet.net, Vol. 2 – Issue 3-September 2001).

I am especially intrigued and inspired by the faithfulness of Dorado, Rivera's faithful Guide Dog who was more than a friend to him in his time of need. Where were Rivera's colleagues? How come none of them risked his/her life to save him? We can learn a great deal from animals. Many animals treat humans with more love and respect than humans receive from their family.

There are many stories of faithfulness and courage of dogs, horses, birds and so on. When I first arrived in the United States, I used to enjoy watching a television program featuring Lassie, a dog that was more powerful than any human rescue squad. Lassie was featured saving sleeping families from a fire, and rescuing babies at the risk of its own life. Would you risk your life to save someone else?

You have the power to train people to treat you the way you want them to treat you. It is the power of personal example. Realign your mind. If you expect others to be faithful to you, you can inspire them by being faithful to them. These days, faithfulness seems to be an empty word. To build a better you, be faithful like Dorado. Show that you care and inspire hope in humanity. Dare to take a risk and save a life. Heal a hurting heart.

SOMETHING TO THINK ABOUT

Can you name five truly faithful friends who will love you in spite of who you are?

Are you as faithful to your friend as Dorado was to Eduardo Rivera?

Collect Royalty for Loyalty

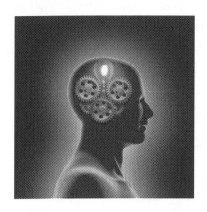

THERE WAS A time when corporations paid big dividends for loyalty. A father would work for a company his entire life, and upon retirement, the company would hire his son to fill his vacancy. In Japan, workers used to form "Think Tanks" and meet on their own time to share innovative ideas to improve the company. Ideas would be presented for management's consideration. The management would reward employees for their contribution, and if an idea was impractical, the employees would be provided an explanation. Things have changed, not only in Japan but globally. Corporations try to buy talents with money and fringe benefits, instead of attracting new employees by their character and excellence in service. Employees, motivated by high wages and perks keep looking for greener pastures, never making a total commitment. Many companies operate on an "At Will" basis, always keeping replacement as one of their choice options. Whatever happened to loyalty?

Many years ago, Elbert Hubbard wrote the following piece on loyalty in the American Business Women's Association newsletter. Hubbard's statement of loyalty is based on common sense and wisdom.

"If you work for a man, in Heaven's name, WORK for him. If he pays you wages which supply you bread and butter, work for him; speak well of him; stand by him and stand by the institution he represents. If put to a pinch, an ounce of loyalty is worth a pound of cleverness. If you must vilify, condemn and eternally disparage—resign your position,

and when you are outside, damn to your heart's content, but as long as you are part of the institution do not condemn it. If you do that, you are loosening the tendrils that are holding you to the institution, and at the first high wind that comes along, you will be uprooted and blown away, and probably will never know the reason why."

I recall a young high school graduate I hired as my secretary when I worked for the government. She was with me for thirteen years. Recognizing her talents and loyalty, I upgraded her position several times. She received three well-paying job offers from outside the agency but declined every one. When I left my position, I recommended her to another large agency that promoted her twice within the first six months. However, mutual commitment between employees and employers is wearing thin these days. Cords that bind employees and employers are basically made up of contractual agreements and bonuses instead of mutual respect and relationships.

Books are full of stories about loyalty of pets and animals to their masters. My father had a horse. If the rider were to fall, it would stop immediately, return home and try to find someone who would follow it to the scene of the accident. When I was a child, I used to have a dog named Moore. He used to give me a ride around the house. I remember once, when Moore and I were on a routine ride, a strange dog tried to bite me. Moore stood on his two front legs and frightened the daylight out of the strange dog. Human beings are supposed to be more intelligent. Are you a loyal worker, friend or a spouse? Can your family count on you? Can workers count on their employers these days? A loyal person does not become disloyal if cheated, deceived, defrauded, or disrespected.

SOMETHING TO THINK ABOUT

Would your family, friends and co-workers consider you a loyal person? Think about it carefully!

Travel Light

THE HEAVIER THE load, the slower will a vehicle run and the more energy it will consume to get to its destination. The airlines monitor the luggage one can carry on the plane in order to ensure safe passage. The international travel policies specify the weight, the size of an object and what you may transport in it.

I learned this principle during one of my trips to India. After paying $85 for excess luggage when I checked my two large suitcases in Los Angeles, I still had five more pieces as carry-ons. My wife helped me carry these pieces into the plane at Los Angeles. However, when I disembarked in New York to change flight to India, I heard a loud announcement, "Only two pieces will be allowed and they must fit under the seat." I was so worried. I did not have enough money to pay for excess baggage again. I looked like a clown with all the excess baggage that relatives had given to me for their friends in India. It was hot. I was sweaty and stressed. People looked at me as though I was crazy. The joy of going home to see my parents in India had been squeezed out and frustration was written all over my face. Finally, per kindness of an airline official, I checked in everything straight to New Delhi, except one book and a camera. I was the happiest traveler.

Most everyone has baggage and some have lots of excess baggage. The baggage is packaged neatly in various forms. For example, divorce, loss of a job, failed business transactions, financial setbacks, and disappointment from the most trusted friends. We are given the night so we can rest and wake up in the morning to face a new day. Our journey of life, too, can become cumbersome if we accumulate excess baggage. I have made up my mind to travel light. Here are a few pieces of excess baggage you must discard in order to ensure a safe and happy trip to your destination.

- Spirit of criticism – It's like spreading cancer along the way.

- The "I can't do it attitude" – It will render you impotent and useless.

- Unforgiving spirit –It will weigh heavily on your heart and slow you down.

- Spirit of revenge – It's like digging our own grave and hurrying to get there.

- Pride and arrogance – It's like walking around with a ton of steel on your back.

- "The get-by spirit" – It's like being an eight-cylinder car but running on only one.

- Irresponsible money management – It's like termites; it will bring down your house.

- Carelessness – It's like sleeping with your eyes open. It has aborted many a journey.

- Laziness – It's a sure way to grow old rapidly and turn your dreams into nightmares.

- Making excuses for your failure– It's like blaming the mirror for the dirt on your face.

- Hanging on to bad relationships – It's like complaining about a migraine but loving it.

- Past negative experiences – It's like digging up dead people to have their funeral again.

- Full-time job and part-time thinking – It's like having an adult body but a juvenile mind.

SOMETHING TO THINK ABOUT

Identify your excess baggage and develop a plan to shed it for your own safety. Don't allow others to load you with their excess baggage.

Take a Trip to Paradise

LIFE IS FULL of challenges and opportunities. There are days you feel on top of the world and days when you feel down in the dumps. There are days when you will say, "What do you expect from a day that begins with waking up." However, the alternative to waking up is a quiet place six feet under ground where silence rules lifelessly. There will be times when you will find yourself at the end of your rope, wishing for a trip to anywhere except where you stand. Our little world is getting noisier, more hectic and stressful. Just remember that nature has arranged to flash a rainbow after the rain. Let me share with you a strategy to cope with life and turn your frustrations into fascinating opportunities for growth.

Before you continue any further, find a quiet place in the office or at home. Sit comfortably on the floor and lean back against the wall. Choose your favorite beach and imagine that you are seated under a palm tree with flowers all around, butterflies hopping from flower to flower and the golden rays of the sun are making the entire shoreline look beautiful. A cool breeze is blowing gently on your face. Close your eyes, put your hands in your lap, and take three deep breaths. Do you feel the air filling your lungs? Now hold each breath for about ten seconds and release it gradually. Do you feel the air leaving the lungs? Take another deep breath and say, "It feels so good to be here in paradise."

Now think as far back in your life as you can remember and recall all the best things that have happened to you – best people you have met, best places you have visited, people who have been a blessing to you, the exciting experiences you have had and things that have made you feel on top of the world. Take another deep breath and whisper to yourself; "It feels so good to visit paradise. I must come here often." Keep viewing the positive videos of your life. If a negative scene comes around, shut off the tape and say, "Today I am viewing only positive tapes." You will discover that there will stand a big mountain of good things that have happened in your life. The negative experiences will seem insignificant. Before you leave the beach, make a resolution to take a trip to paradise as often as possible.

On your journey to paradise, you will come across many who have been to the land of regrets, singing the song, "What could have been." What could have, should have, would have, may have, might have, ought to have been is an exercise in futility. It will leave you stranded in a waste land with other hopeful but idle minds. You must realign your mind and take a trip to paradise. You can repeat this exercise as often as you wish. Eventually your mind will get in the habit of focusing only on the positives. You know what they say, "It's not good to make a mountain out of a molehill." Take it easy and don't sweat the small stuff.

SOMETHING TO THINK ABOUT

The mind has a unique characteristic. It develops a dynamic relationship with whatever you feed it. Train your mind to focus on the paradise experiences of your life.

 # Have Patience It's a Fountain of Peace

PATIENCE IS POWER! It reveals the depth of your wisdom and the strength of your character. Impatience, on the other hand, is the offspring of impetuousness and the older sister of foolishness. There is never a good reason to be impatient. Impatience pays poor wages. Impatient people, unable to wait to receive their just reward, settle for far less than they deserve.

Let me share one of my own experiences with impatience. I had moved into a new apartment. I needed to buy some drapes for my living room. I was single, so my supervisor and his wife offered to help me with selecting the drapes. We found lovely drapes at the Broadway. They were the right color and perfect for my little apartment. As I was taking the drapes to the cash register, the sales clerk leaned over and whispered to me, "If you can wait to take the delivery on Sunday (two days later), they will be marked down 25%." What do you think was my response to the gracious sales clerk? "No, I would rather have these today." Talk about being impatient! I was an impatient fool. Today, I am willing to wait for a month or two if I can save just 10%.

A very few have the patience to discover the true power of patience. Imagine if Mahatma Gandhi had given in to impatience and lost his temper! He would have lost his charisma and his sense of mission. The British could never disturb the foundation of his power – patience. What if Martin Luther King Jr. had become impatient and given up because the wheels of justice moved too slowly for him to realize his dream! A patient person is mightier than a general with an army of a million armed soldiers. I am patiently building my patience. How about you?

Impatience not only leads one to make unwise decisions, it also compromises relationships. Have you ever wished you could take back your words or renegotiate the decision you made in haste? Impatience comes in many shapes and forms. Impatient people are like the unwise poultry farmer who counts his chickens before the eggs are hatched. Impatient people:

- Don't allow people to express themselves. They jump in and complete their sentences.

- Spit out the first idea or word that comes to their mind. They are poor listeners.

- Forfeit gifts, bargains, blessings, and the honor that come to those who wait.

- Don't think of alternatives to improve outcomes in resolving conflicts.

- Cannot wait to settle the matter, even if it means getting a raw deal.

- Ruin relationships by their unwillingness to listen and learn.

SOMETHING TO THINK ABOUT

To build your patience, you must be unselfish. When tempted to blurt out, ask yourself three questions: If I do not have my way, will I get arrested? Will I die? Will waiting preserve or ruin my relationship? Wisdom builds patience. Wisdom is to know a lot and hold your tongue.

Hate a Few Things Passionately

I LIKE PEOPLE and love working with them. I can even get along with the devil. In fact, I get special strength when I encounter someone who is obnoxious. Adrenalin begins to gush around in my body and kicks me into high gear to take on a challenge to make friends with a person to whom most people would award a one-way ticket to Siberia. However, I passionately detest certain behaviors that compromise our effectiveness. You may want to make up your own list. If you don't like such behaviors when displayed by others, chances are that others, too, don't like these when displayed by you.

Elephant Teeth: Just like some elephants have two sets of teeth, one set to chew and one set to display, some people are two-faced. They smile to your face, while in their hearts they wish you were dead. It is our basic human right that we get what we see. I hate people being phony! Don't you? In pursuit of excellence, you say what you mean and mean what you say. People shouldn't have to guess where you stand. Take a stand. Don't be a marshmallow!

Unforgiving Spirit: One of the greatest injustices we can render to one another, and especially to our own growth, is to harbor grudges and rob one another of the opportunity to start over. Unless we forgive, we don't really live! Ignore a few things. It is said that "Forgiveness is the fragrance that flowers exude when they are trampled upon." When we learn to forgive, we become focused on our life's mission and don't allow petty issues to detour us from our goal.

Go easy on people so they will be easy on you.

Pride: Pride is the first step on the road that leads to the land of self-destruction. The Good Book advises that we take a back seat at a banquet and let the host call us to the front, instead of taking the front seat, and have the host ask us to vacate it for a more honorable guest. Put others first and you will be propelled forward and stand head and shoulders above the ordinary people.

Jealousy: Displaying even the slightest sign of jealousy is a clear declaration of our incompetence to attain what others rightfully have earned. If you want to look taller than your neighbor, get a stool to stand on, instead of cutting his legs off to make you look taller.

Lust: Men, sexual impropriety will do you in. Treat every female as your daughter, sister or mother. Ladies, treat every male as your brother.

Greed & Gluttony: Greed and gluttony often lead to indigestion and ills that later require radical actions to get your life in order. Keep these two beasts under check.

Silent Treatment: Resorting to the silent treatment to express your displeasure with others is a cowardly way to manage your human relationships. Grow up and take charge of your life. Deal with disagreements in an agreeable way. Resolve issues and clear your path to your destination.

Gossip: If people spoke the truth and had the power to stand behind their word, they would not have to sneak behind their friends, family and colleagues to spit venom. Don't say anything that you would be afraid to read in the local newspaper. Gossip is akin to assassination.

Laziness: The time clock keeps on ticking. If you use every second effectively, you will add value to every minute of your life. If you use each minute creatively, your hours will be more valuable. If every hour is utilized carefully, your life will be purposeful and productive. If you start something, see it to the finish line. If you start a conversation, learn to end it on time before it gets boring or slips into an unproductive zone. If you are not lazy, you will have no regrets at the end of your journey.

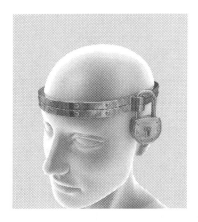

Working with the Walking Dead

I HAVE BEEN working in the market place for over four decades. I used to have a colleague who often joked by saying, "I love my work I can sit and watch it for hours." Some are allergic to the four-letter word "WORK." It makes them break out in hives. I have heard every conceivable name given to describe such employees. Let me introduce you to some of them:

"Day Dreamers."	"Happy Wanderers."	"Open Eye Sleeper."	"Clock Watchers."
"Walking Dead."	"Sleeping Giants."	"Out-to-Lunch."	"Straw Head."
"Not-all-There."	"Sleeping Heads."	"Dead Wood."	"Meat Head."
"Man ana Mind."	"Absent Minded."	"Has Been."	"Cutie Booty."

In my career, I have encountered almost all of the people listed above. When I first began my work for the government, I had a colleague who specialized in "shortstops." Every hour he would visit all the offices within my unit asking everyone "How is it going?" Some employees got so fed up with his hourly interruptions that when he would ask, "How is it going," the usual reply was "It's not going." Then there was a lady who would dress up in her graceful long Victorian dress and go from room to room greeting her colleagues at least twice a day. She was labeled "Happy Wanderer." I asked her what her mission was in making trips around the building. "I just try to cheer people up," she responded. I asked her if she would be willing to delegate that role to her supervisor so she could get her own work done. I had to diplomatically have her relinquish her "cheerleading" so her colleagues could have a little peace of mind.

Then there was Sue. She specialized in keeping track of who is dating whom, who was getting divorced, who was having a baby, who was going on vacation, who had a quarrel with her mother-in-law, whose doggy was having puppies, who was not getting along with her live-in boyfriend and so on. I had to work with her on her job description so she would have something to do other than being a reporter for the "National Enquirer."

Bad employees come in all shapes and sizes and bearing all sorts of labels. However, the bottom line is that they are lifeless. They are termites that eat your organization from the inside. If you have enough of such people, you don't need outside enemies to do you in. They are the "dead wood" that your predecessor did not have the guts to eliminate. They are the cancerous cells that are sucking your organization of its lifeblood. If you cannot mend their behavior, you must have the guts to end such negative relationships to safeguard your company's future. Don't delay. Take action!

SOMETHING TO THINK ABOUT

You must come alive and bring these "deadbeats" to life or you will go down the chute with them. Build a better you so none of the labels listed above would fit you.

Think of ten ways you can infuse life in your lifeless colleagues.

Myths about Motivation

TO BE MOTIVATED by forces outside of us is a myth. External incentives provide a temporary push to get people out of their parking position. However, they are short-lived and have marginal results. Consider a fancy powerful sports car that boasts of winning races but its battery cannot hold a charge. It always requires jumper cables to get it started. What if no one comes that way with jumper cables? Think of a clock that prizes itself for keeping accurate time, come rain or shine, but it requires someone to wind it each morning. What will happen if someone forgets to wind it? How about a champion greyhound that can run faster than the fastest cheetah but it would not get going unless someone prompted it with an electric shock!

If your people continuously require incentives before they can step up to the plate, you might be surrounding yourself with the wrong people. They are like a wheelbarrow that needs pushing. Maybe they are not the right people for the job. External incentives can create an "air of appreciation," an environment that signals the employees that their good work is being noted and appreciated, but it is not the main booster vitamin or a steady diet of champions.

I define motivation as a fire in our belly that totally consumes us until we land at our destination. It is an intense love for someone or something that arouses an unquenchable thirst or passion to propel us toward our goal. For example, a drowning man yearns for a breath of fresh air and catches even a straw with hopes it will sustain him. The internal stimulus grips his heart and drives him to action. He does not need a lecture on motivation. It ignites a fire that cannot be quenched. Is there fire burning in your belly for something? If the spark is still lit, a small amount of lighter fluid may make it glow. However, if the fire is out, a tank of gasoline would be a wasted exercise. Many people are like a musical doll that needs someone to wind it before it can sing.

Many cheat themselves by performing like an automobile when they can fly like a supersonic jet. I have seen many sales persons who operate like a car on one cylinder because the boss does not give them a bonus on top of their commission. External rewards should not be a condition for us to do our best, to achieve our best, or to be the best. By depending on external cues to get us going, we deprive ourselves of the rich reservoir of resources within us and cheat ourselves. Doing our best and tasting excellence in the work of our hands should be a reward in itself. External cues are like clouds; they may or may not show up. Finally, people who are motivated only by money are selling themselves way too short.

The real incentive to move us forward should always be what leads us closer to our dream destination. Have you charted your course? Have you decided where you would like to land at the end of your journey? Do you have a map for the road? Have you calculated the cost? Are you prepared to pay the price? Have you inventoried your inner strength and your external support system needed for your road to success? What motivates you to get up each day? If achieving excellence is your goal, you don't need any external motivation. The fire within your belly will make you restless until you have given your all to get where you want to go.

SOMETHING TO THINK ABOUT

Do you tend to wait for an outside force to get you going? Take time to assess your purpose in life and you will have all the motivation you need to get you going.

Be a Good Fruit Tree Not a Fruitcake

PEOPLE ARE LIKE trees. They stay green and grow, or they dry out and are uprooted. A healthy tree grows new leaves every season or stays green year around. A tree bears flowers and fruit and multiplies itself to grow more fruit trees. In order for the tree to be healthy, it must receive water and food on time. A healthy tree grows strong roots so it may stand firm when storms and harsh weather beat on it. Scientists have observed that when certain pine trees are seeded, and the young seed is sprouting, it has so much power that if a rock is in its path, it will split the rock. It is no mystery that a healthy tree produces healthy fruit.

Many people, instead of being healthy fruit trees, are fruitcakes. Seasons come and seasons go, but they do not grow new leaves. They learn nothing new. They live on their past knowledge that is outdated and outmoded. They do not feed on new food. Soon they run out of ideas and keep spinning their wheels. They have shallow roots. The first wind that blows their way uproots them. They abandon their goals at the slightest resistance. Postponed thinking, lack of planning, hanging on to dysfunctional old ideas and inability to seek help keeps them slaves to poor performance. Eventually, they give up the ghost and settle for lowlands of mediocrity and "get-by" mentality. They do just enough so that they will not earn a "pink slip," but not enough so that they could be featured as exemplary employees. But you are different! You are building a better you! Remember, if a fruit tree could grow to be 50 feet tall, it would never stop until it reaches its full potential. Keep focused. You can accomplish whatever your heart desires.

As discussed earlier, a tree takes in carbon dioxide and gives out oxygen, a life- saving gas. Without oxygen we would die. Similarly, on our journey of life we need one another for survival. We need to develop a supportive and nurturing atmosphere around us. We must add life to people wherever we go. We must add value to whatever we touch. Imagine this world full of people like trees that are green, full of flowers, and loaded with fruit. The true fruit of our life is seen in the life we generate in others. When the lives of people around us become better and more valuable because of our investment in them, we become the fruitful tree that has multiplied itself to feed future generations.

The next time you walk around a garden or an orchard, take a look at the trees more carefully and see how your life may resemble the fruitful trees. If you notice an unhealthy tree, study to discover what messed up its growth and learn how it could be revived. Perhaps there would a lesson or two on how to regenerate your own roots and grow. Perhaps it would give you some hints on how to reseed your hopes and dreams, bring flowers and bear fruit to bless yourself and others.

SOMETHING TO THINK ABOUT

Plant a fruit tree in your backyard and watch it grow, and bear leaves, flowers and fruit.

Select a fruit tree of your choice and study all you can about how to care for it, and then apply those lessons to your life.

Take This Job and Love It

NOTE: YOUR WORK is your art. If you love your art, you will not allow yourself to offer to the world any less than you can deliver. If you deliver the best you can, your love for your art will grow. As your love for your art grows, you will add value to everyone and everything you touch. Here are seven questions to help you determine what is expected of you in the practice of your art. These questions can be applied also to one's personal or family life.

1.

What exactly do I do here?

2.

What is its value to the agency?

3.

How do I contribute to the bottom line?

4.

How do I contribute to make

my colleagues successful?

5.

If I leave, will I be missed?

6.

Will the agency replace me?

7.

What will be my legacy?

Why Become Just Anybody When You Can Become Somebody Special?

L ET ME INTRODUCE to you Jose Sanchez. Jose works as a Finance Manager for Family Motors in Bakersfield, California. He is one of the most sincere and down-to-earth men I have ever met. One day I asked Jose to share with me how he became so disciplined an individual. Here is Jose' response. "When I was in second grade, I did not like to go to school. One day I told my mother that I was not feeling well. I would like to stay home. My mother focused her piercing eyes on me and said, 'If you are not going to go to school, maybe you want to go with me. I will be working all day, picking vegetables in the cold and chilly weather. I am not even sure I will make enough to feed you all by the end of the day. All day I will be shivering and listening to the farm owner shouting, 'rapido, rapido' (hurry up). You can come with me or go to school. No good son of mine is going to cut school. At school they are going to feed you and teach you. You will be in a warm place. Now listen to me and some day you will be somebody.'"

"I listened to my mother and went to school. From second grade on, until I graduated from college, I did not miss even one class, and neither did I ever report late to school. I have been working for Family Motors for nine years. I have never called in sick and I have never been late to work." Wow! How many people have such a perfect record? Jose dresses like a professional, speaks like a professional and works like a professional.

Jim Rohm, one of the foremost people builders in America, tells the story of Abraham Lincoln in one of his tapes. Before Lincoln's mother died, she called him close to her and whispered, "I am leaving. Go and be somebody." Laura Morsch, CareerBuilder.com, featured an article on February 3, 2005, "Celebrity Career Setbacks." Here is what she wrote about Lincoln, "Abe Lincoln failed in business in 1831 and again in 1833. In the meantime, he ran for state legislator and lost. His sweetheart died in 1835, and he had a nervous breakdown the next year. He lost the nomination to Congress in 1843, was defeated again for Congress in 1848 and 1855 and lost the vice-presidency of the United States in 1856. Then he ran for Senator in 1858 and lost."

The man who was to dominate human history forever, was beaten down by his opponents and his circumstances many times, but nothing could defeat his spirit. The words of his dying mother were more powerful than the thunder of opposing forces. In 1860 Abe Lincoln was elected President of the United States to make history by freeing the soul of America and all mankind from hatred and injustice. His voice of reason still echoes throughout the world and calls all sane people to stand firm and tall against everything that threatens human freedom and gives rise to selfishness over sacrificial service. Although assassinated, he still lives in the hearts and minds of all freedom-loving people and influences human life and politics everywhere.

SOMETHING TO THINK ABOUT

A person who has resolved to be somebody, is stronger than an army, mightier than a mountain, and his spirit can never be dampened by a million wet blankets. Nothing can keep you down unless you allow it. Now, go and "Be Somebody."

Always Wear Clean Underwear And Socks without Holes

MY GRANDMOTHER WAS 103 years old when she died. However, her voice never faded. She spoke with authority and commanded respect. She especially loved my father and had extra special love for me. When I was a child, she often bathed me and scrubbed me real well to make sure that all the dirt was gone. We did not have running water, not to mention that the water temperature never rose above 50 degrees. I often felt that my bones would be frozen and my jaws would fall off by just shivering.

After a thorough cleanup, my grandmother would yell and say, "Now make sure you have clean underwear and socks without holes." Grandmother always INSPECTED what she EXPECTED. She would hold my head in both of her hands, kiss me on my forehead, look into my eyes and ask, "Are you wearing clean underwear and socks without holes?" There were times when I did not see the importance of what she demanded. I would quickly yell, "Who is going to see my underwear or socks? No one will know what I am wearing anyway." Hearing that ridiculous response she would yell back, "You are not wearing clean underwear or socks for someone else. You are doing it for you and you know it if they are clean and without holes. Now, go on to school and hurry back."

I have never forgotten my grandmother's love and concern for me, especially, her advice of wearing clean underwear and socks without holes. I have often thought of the significance of what she lovingly demanded of me. I realize the value of her advice more now than when I first heard it. I realize that she was laying a foundation for building my character by teaching me the principle that we must keep clean even the part of our life that no one may ever discover.

There is a song that goes something like this, "If you could read my mind love…" What if people could really read what is brewing in our mind? In the movie, "What Women Really Want," Mel Gibson stuns women when he talks to them about the thoughts that have been circling in their minds. While what goes on in our mind is a private matter, it is vital that we guard our mind and be selective in what is stored in it. Even if no one can read our mind, the results of the ideas hatched in our mind are eventually an open book for everyone to read.

Would you be proud if people saw the list of the books you read, the way you spend your money and the way you use your leisure time? Would you feel comfortable if your children watched the movies you watch, or listen to the music you enjoy when no one is with you? Would you be proud if your family, friends or neighbors knew the thoughts in your mind? What if people really knew what you mutter under your breath when you are upset? The real person is made up of thoughts, habits, and actions we take when no one is watching. What people see is often prompted but one's social, cultural and environmental cues. The true beliefs, values and attitude are formed by what we do in private. This eventually surfaces as our real self.

SOMETHING TO THINK ABOUT

Are you wearing clean underwear and socks without holes? What does it mean to you?

Seek Wisdom over Enthusiasm

A WISE MAN once said, "Wisdom is better than strength, it is better than weapons of war." The word 'KNOWLEDGE' has in it the word "KNOW." The word "WISDOM" has in it the word 'DO.' Unless what we know adds value to something or someone, all we have is just a bunch of irrelevant facts. We may try to impress others and embarrass ourselves. During a summer vacation I learned that wisdom is far more valuable than enthusiasm.

I had just completed my junior year at college and I was feeling quite content with what I had accomplished. I was the first one in my family to go to college. We were having a serious discussion on a topic when, all of sudden, I caught myself spitting out a lot of facts to win the argument, and with great enthusiasm, I might add! Realizing that I did not score points with anyone, I felt quite stupid and sad. My father, who is my mentor, looked at me and comforted me by saying, "Don't worry. Young people usually have a lot of enthusiasm but not enough wisdom." He politely put me in my place and taught me to use my mind instead of my mouth. He taught me to listen, analyze, and politely but firmly shed light on the issue at hand. Don't try to get even with people just to win an argument. Here are a few scenarios to help you exercise wisdom over enthusiasm.

- You are at a party and a loud-mouth insults you. You get an intense urge to cut him to size and put him in his place. What would be the wisest thing to do? ***Ignore it.*** The person is on a slippery slope. Don't stop him. Let him go down the chute. You cannot save him.

- Your boss insults you in front of your colleagues. It kindles your anger. You want to tell him where to go. Miss Wisdom pops up and whispers to you… "The boss is making a fool of himself. You have already won the hearts of your colleagues. Silence is golden. Unless you have another job offer, stay calm, and stay cool. Deal with it later."

- A colleague is taking the credit for the work you have done. He is bragging about it at a company party. You want to set the record straight and embarrass him in front of his fiancée. Wisdom comes rushing in and says… "Tell Mr. Loudmouth that you would like to meet with him later to discuss this project." Chances are that others already know that you are the real hero. You need not stoop to his level.

Wisdom is the key that opens our eyes and allows us to see positive alternatives to negative and hurtful things people throw our way. Wisdom will save us from being distracted by detours that lead people to expend precious time on arguing about insignificant and meaningless matters.

It is reported that during his election, his rival Douglas accused Mr. Lincoln of being a two-faced person. Lincoln, instead of insulting back, simply replied, "Tell me, if I had two faces, would I be wearing the one I am wearing?" Everyone laughed and Lincoln won the hearts of his audience. Wise people don't make fools of themselves. They always take the high road.

SOMETHING TO THINK ABOUT

When challenged and tempted to retaliate, use wisdom. Exercise self-control.

Wash Your
Wagon Often

POSTED AT THE door of a dry cleaning store in Fresno, California was a sign, "Wash Your Wagon." At times I have seen messages written on the windows of dirty vehicles, "Wash Me, Clean Me." My father usually says, "Clean cars run better." In my neighborhood there was a man who used to park his wagon full of garbage right in front of his house. That wagon was an eyesore in the neighborhood. The wagon was loaded with old furniture, bald tires, broken pottery, old clothes, a rusty washing machine and many black bags filled with…who knows what. When I went jogging by the place, I often heard neighbors stand, stare at the old wagon, sigh and whisper, "Why does he not get rid of the garbage and wash his wagon?"

As I have walked by my neighbor's wagon, I have often thought of another wagon – the human mind. We all have this wagon. It is amazing how many have their wagon loaded with old miserable memories. They keep the wagon loaded with negative experiences they had years ago. They still remember being slighted when they were in high school or college. They cannot forget being left off the invitation list of Aunt Agatha's sixtieth birthday party fifteen years ago. They still remember when their spouse forgot their wedding anniversary. Their wagon is overloaded with hurt feelings, unhealed wounds, broken promises of days gone by, and many other unpleasant memories. The wagon has been full and parked for so long that within minutes of conversation their friends can smell the foul odors. The stench of storing all the clutter from the past keeps them preoccupied with unhappy memories. They remain slaves to the events that occurred decades ago. Although they think they are independent, in fact, people who hurt them years ago are still in control of their lives. Although disappointed for not having made much headway in life, they comfort themselves by blaming people and poor circumstances.

To keep the wagon loaded and refusing to dump it is like refusing to flush the toilet when the bowl is full. Garbage begins to smell after a few days. I often advise people not to sleep with their wagon full of garbage or they may wake up stinking and ruin their entire next day. It is good to empty the mind and recharge it for achieving what we were created to achieve.

One of my colleagues once shared his secret of coming to work with his wagon totally clean. He told me that before he leaves his house, he goes to the garbage bin and pretends that he is taking off his cap, gown and overshoes and dumping them into the garbage can. Then he dusts his feet and gets into his car. He has done this routine for years to get his mind free of any unpleasant thoughts prior to coming to work. I think that is a neat tradition. What is in your wagon? Have you cleaned it and washed it lately? Do you have room now to store new and beautiful gifts from friends and family? If your children were to look inside your wagon, would they find in it anything that might hurt them? If your children were to store in their wagon the things you store in your wagon, would they be able to travel light? Are you proud of what you store in your wagon (mind)? If people could see inside your wagon, would you be embarrassed? I want my wagon to be clean and washed every day. How about you?

SOMETHING TO THINK ABOUT

Do you have the courage to empty your wagon of all undesirable things? Make a resolution to keep your wagon clean and ready to store new gifts.

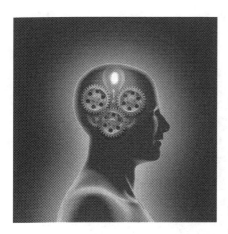

Hang Loose and Stay Cool: Be a Solution Person

ONCE I WAS working for a corporation comprised of twelve different businesses owned by one person. Among the many hats I wore, it was my joy to oversee customer care. Those who were unhappy were referred to me. There were times when people would enter my room fuming with anger and expressing it with choice vocabulary that I was not accustomed to hear. While other managers dreaded to see angry clients entering the showroom, I was literally delighted to see such individuals because I knew that I was going to have the opportunity to put a smile on their faces. I could hardly wait for them to be referred to me by the receptionist. I usually got animated hearing the customers' stories. I used the two cardinal principles my Dad taught me "Stay calm and don't get angry." When it came to customer care, I was the "solution man" for the company. Let me share the plan that worked miraculously for me.

1. **Thank Them.** No matter what people say, always thank them for taking the time to bring the matter to your attention. It shows that they love the company. Most disgruntled customers would tell twenty-two other customers not to do business with you. The customers who cuss and share their feelings are helping you improve your business.

2. **Empathize.** After the people have spewed venom, I generally say "You are not half as angry as I would be if I were in your shoes." This cools them down immediately.

3. **Commend Them.**   Tell them that you are glad that they felt comfortable in expressing themselves in the way they thought appropriate. This takes away the guilt and the anger.

4. **Listen With Your Heart**. Pay full attention to the other side of the story. Request them to calmly explain the problem so you may be helpful to them.

5. **Explain Your Side of the Story.**   Take the time to help them understand the problem from your perspective. Since you listened to them, they are likely to listen to you.

6. **Make a Commitment to Resolve the Problem.** Finally, take personal responsibility to resolve the problem and seek their cooperation. Remember, being a solution person does not mean having your way. It means creating a proposition acceptable to both parties. Focus on building a two-way bridge.

I have followed this six-step process that has resulted in absolutely amazing success. Most people feel guilty for getting angry and blowing their top. Be a solution person. Take responsibility. Don't make excuses when things go wrong. Don't try to find an "escape goat." Hang loose and stay cool. These principles will make you an unbeatable negotiator. Nothing is more important in life than peace of mind. Peace of mind is the result of living and working in harmony with your inner self and the people around you. Create synergy.

SOMETHING TO THINK ABOUT

Write down twenty ways you can improve your listening skills. Select a recent incident where you were in conflict with someone and think about three alternatives that could have improved the solution.

Tips On Solving Problems

Don't try to defeat the other person

Develop shared solutions

Don't look for shortcuts

Hold people responsible

Listen with your heart

Don't listen to gossip

Do your homework

Don't be in a hurry

Stay cool and calm

Ask for feedback

Avoid detours

Expect results

Be agreeable

Be pleasant

Be Proactive – Build a Fence

T HERE WAS A big hill in the middle of an old town. In the evening, lovers would go up the hill, hold hands, look at the stars and stroll around in romance. Every now and then, a couple would fall off the cliff. The City Fathers had stationed an ambulance at the bottom of the hill to rush the injured to a nearby hospital emergency room. This had been the routine until a young boy asked his father, why doesn't the city build a fence on top of the hill instead of parking an ambulance at the bottom?

It may sound strange, however, but that's how many people manage their lives. They wait for things to go wrong before they take any action. Many employers I am sure have heard the statement, "Squeaky-wheel gets the grease." In other words, people wait until they are forced to take the action. This, in life, is known as reaction. It is usually too little, too late.

I love playing chess. It is a great game. It teaches the player to anticipate the moves of the opponent and stay ahead a few moves. In chess, one must always protect the king. The player is prepared to sacrifice all other pieces in order to save the king. Life is more than a game of chess. It requires us to plan and anticipate the results before acting. We must live in the future because the future is being designed by our present actions.

In pursuit of excellence, one must become proactive instead of waiting for things to fall apart and then scramble to find a quick fix.

- If you know the toilet bowl is stuffed, clear it. Don't wait until it overflows.

- If you know your actions are driving your spouse or your child insane, make amends. Don't wait for a second opinion.

- If you know the gas tank is on reserve, fill it. It would be foolish to keep driving until it runs dry and leaves you stranded on the road to nowhere.

- If you know your performance is slipping, take action. Don't wait for a "pink slip" to motivate you.

- If you find your pants, skirt or a blouse is an inch too tight, get a plan and get in shape. Don't wait until you need size 44 to go on a crash diet.

- If something is giving you a headache, mend it or end it. Don't wait until it you develop a migraine.

- If you know your brakes are squeaking, it would not be prudent to wait to replace them until its time to replace the rotors or the drums.

- If you know that saying a simple "Sorry" would fix the problem, don't wait to settle it until your neighbor hauls you into court.

Attempting to change things after the will is written and the person is dead, brings regrets. In pursuit of building a better you, think ahead. It was not raining when Noah built the ark!

SOMETHING TO THINK ABOUT

Take an inventory of your life and see if there is a need to build a fence somewhere.

Do you concur that the cost for reaction is far greater than that of action taken in time?

Be Flexible

S OME PEOPLE ARE afraid of traveling by plane, but not me. I enjoy flying. If I had my way, I would grow wings so I could fly. Whenever I do fly, I request a window seat from where I can see the wings of the plane. When I was writing this chapter, I was flying from Kansas City to my home in California. I occupied seat 26A in an American Airlines plane MD 80. The plane was cruising at the speed of 500 miles an hour, 28,000 feet in the sky. As the plane took off, I saw its wings turning in and out, adjusting to the speed of the wind. I recall once when I was flying from Ontario, California to Lake Tahoe, the plane encountered a severe storm, wind, rain and even some snow. However, the plane was able to stay on course and we landed safely. Have you ever wondered what helps these giant silver birds stay on course? The secret is in their wings. The wings are designed to be flexible. If its wings were not flexible, faced with the power of the wind, the wings would break and the plane would crash. There is a great lesson for life here.

On our journey of life, FLEXIBILITY is one of the most important and the most powerful tools to help us succeed. In real life, most people would rather give up than give in occasionally. If I have discovered anything in life, it is the fact that things don't always go my way. Things change. People change their minds, resources I expect do not always materialize, weather does not cooperate, and in some cases, I find myself unprepared for the challenge. The easiest route to take would be to abandon the dream and blame the world. Whenever the winds have shifted their direction, I have fallen back on the advice of my mentor who taught me to "REVIEW, RETHINK, REGROUP, REDESIGN, REGENERATE and REDIRECT your energy."

Flexibility does not refer to compromising our values. Flexibility demonstrates our ability to evaluate other ideas and viewpoints and adjust our perspective in light of a new reality. At home, flexibility may help us to listen to our family with greater attention. At the office it may help us to welcome feedback from colleagues and supervisors. In the market place, flexibility may help us to create a win-win climate and improve our business. In our friendship circle, flexibility may make us better team players. I am sure you have encountered many people in your life who believed that their way was the only right way. People do not enjoy the company of such individuals. I would rather be flexible than insist on my own way and be proven wrong.

In the art of building a better you, one must realign his/her mind and develop synergy. We must listen with a heart to learn and a willingness to give a serious look at ideas different from our own. We don't have to always agree, but the law of progress dictates that we evaluate other perspectives and remain willing to change our minds if it would improve things. Inflexible people are often forced to abort their journey prematurely and at destinations they did not foresee. A rubber band is flexible; that's why it can hold a lot more within its grasp. Flexibility is the foundation of learning and growing.

It does not pay to be dogmatic. Rigidity freezes creativity and potential progress. Our way may be the only way as we know it; however, that may not be the best way. It is prudent to be humble and submit to learn from others. Be flexible. Anticipate and accept new ideas. Listen to others' point of view and work hard to make others' ideas work.

SOMETHING TO THINK ABOUT

Think of a person who is inflexible and write down the lessons you can learn from his/her way of thinking and acting.

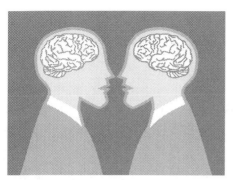

Don't Major
In Minors

THINK OF A microscope. It magnifies little things. When you are looking through a microscope, you are not looking for the big picture. You are trying to look for things that naked human eyes cannot see. Similarly, people who micromanage are oblivious to the BIG PICTURE. They forget the overall purpose of things. Instead, they begin to major in minors and waste precious resources that may result in less than 2-3% of the overall productivity in a system. Be aware of such nitpickers, naggers, super-specialists, and perfectly imperfect people. They believe that unless they keep needling the workers, the workers will slack off, forget their assignments, and do things only half-way. They think that employees will not return just dividends for the owner's investment. This is known as Theory X. It shows a lack of trust in people and a lack of respect for their skills and talents. Such a belief devalues the team members. It makes them feel that watchdogs are roaming around hoping to catch them doing something wrong. It gives them the impression that the hound dogs are anxious to pounce, maim and demoralize workers. Here are some suggestions to help you focus on the big picture while bringing out the best in your team.

1.

Clarify Expectations

2.

Delegate with Authority

3.

Provide Adequate Tools

4.

Coach & Ask for Feedback

5.

Hold People Responsible

6.

Praise your Team in Public

7.

Give More Responsibility

8.

**Catch People Doing Something Approximately
Right and Commend Them**

9.

Be Accessible, Observe and Support

Be a Good Neighbor

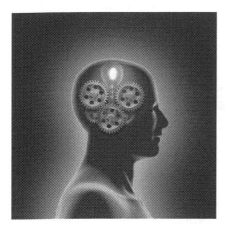

WHEN YOU PURSUE the path of "Building a Better You," you become a citizen of the universe. You become the "Trustee" and the Guardian of the "soul" of all mankind. Your mission expands far beyond your backyard. You become color-blind and cannot see ethnic or racial labels designed to segregate and separate families, communities and countries. Your life takes on a new mission to one big global human family. You discover a special meaning in service to everyone who meets you on your journey of life. You begin to see everyone in need as your neighbor.

If I were to walk your neighborhood and ask those who live within four blocks of your home, will they acknowledge that they know you? Will they recognize your name? Will they remember you as a neighbor who is very friendly and helpful? Will they be able to talk about a specific incident when you went out of your way to add value to their life? Will they call you their friend? Will they recall collaborating with you on some specific community cause to benefit the neighborhood? If a natural disaster were to attack your community, will your neighbors feel that they can count on you for support? I hope your answer to all of these questions is an emphatic "yes." That's what neighbors are all about.

I am very fortunate to be living in a neighborhood where we exchange our addresses and telephone numbers, know one another by name and keep in touch in case of emergencies or special events. My neighbors Gary and Lynn are SUPER NEIGHBORS. Gary is a retired banker. He takes it upon himself to keep us all updated. In fact, he keeps track even of the "city trash pick- up days." If a neighbor goes on vacation, Gary offers to pick up the mail, drag the huge trash drum to the street curb so that the city can haul it away. Gary watches over our homes when we are away and is happy to water our plants and even mow the yard. Gary and I have very differing political views but we are happy to be neighbors. Gary and Lynn are real family folks. Every evening they open their garage, put lawn chairs out and sit and chat for hours. It makes me feel homesick for India where I grew up. It gives one a real sense of community.

Neighbors working together can perform miracles. Bakersfield, known as the "All America" city is located 90 miles north of Los Angeles. The City with a highly diverse population has been organized into "Neighborhood Partnerships." Health, social, spiritual and economic leaders work together to pool resources and build neighborhoods. When I worked for the Kern County Department of Public Health, I had the opportunity to collaborate with these Neighborhood Partnerships to bolster the childhood immunization levels from 29% to over 80% in five years. Physicians, nurses, service clubs collaborated with the County Health Department to improve child health. People working together can accomplish what money cannot. Be a good neighbor. Make a difference!

SOMETHING TO THINK ABOUT

Have you observed your neighborhood lately? What about the unjustified rate hikes in utilities, drug trafficking, crime, vandalism or just neglect of the elderly? Get involved with health and social service agencies to build stronger and safer communities. Make a difference. You can!

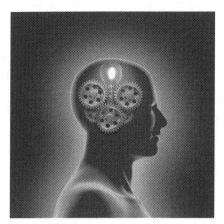

Ten Small Things That Make a Big Difference

SHOW KINDNESS: PRACTICE kindness, especially toward those who are unkind to you. It may not seem logical or reasonable but return kindness for rudeness anyway, even toward those who wish you were dead. Rude people have a very low opinion of themselves. Be kind to them and you will not only heal their hurting heart but also heal the earth.

Praise Others Liberally: In our culture, people are not used to hearing good things said about them. When praised, they either over-compensate for the hidden yearning for praise, or they become allergic to compliments. There is the worst in the best of us and the best in the worst of us. Search hard and find something nice in people and affirm them.

Forgive Without Being Asked: The hardest thing for little people is to admit that they may be wrong. They offend and then defend their actions as though their life depended on proving themselves "right." They have a tough time to eat humble pie and ask forgiveness, even if their offensive behavior is as clear as daylight. It is a sign of greatness to take the first step, forgive, forget and reach out and make the little people feel big.

Have an Attitude of Gratitude: An attitude of gratitude will open doors for you that otherwise will remain shut. Look for the silver lining in every cloud instead of a cloud in every silver lining. Grateful and optimistic people live longer and happier lives.

Give Cheerfully: There is no better way to heal your soul and pack happiness into your bones than to lend a helping hand to someone in need. It is easier to give money than to get personally involved. If all you do is to give money, you are cheating yourself of great blessings that would revive and revitalize your life. Be part of something bigger than yourself.

Practice Wisdom: Wisdom is mightier than the sword. It is the art of applying what we know to help others achieve their maximum potential. It helps us match our deed and creed. It will keep us from stumbling into the dark and tripping over mountains of our follies. Wisdom will help us speak less, listen more and control our anger.

Admire Small Things: Over 95% of life's joys are made up of little things. By ignoring small wonders we often cheat ourselves of the greatest pleasures in life. Think of the happiest times of your life and you will discover that most of your own happiness came in small packages.

Be Money Wise: You don't have to be a genius to discover that the road to unhappiness is paved by spending more than you make. If you make a $100, live on $70, save $20 and give $10 to a charity of your choice. If you live within your means, your days will be many and happy.

Take Care of Your Body: Most people treat their cars better than their bodies. Regular exercise, healthy diet, refraining from alcohol and tobacco products, keeping your weight down, getting 7 to 8 hours of sleep daily, practicing meditation, yoga, getting massages, and relaxing are just a few simple things to stay in good health.

Live By Priorities: Put first things first. Connect with Higher Power. Don't ignore the needs of your family, get involved in your community and while you work hard to make a living, don't forget to build a life.

Keep Life Simple

MANY YEARS AGO I heard the story of a young man who was in a special school to become a spy for his country. He graduated and was assigned to infiltrate and disband a foreign spy ring. He was blindfolded, put in a plane and at midnight dropped in a foreign land. He was given a map and the address of an experienced spy who was to mentor him. He found a large complex and looked for the mentor by the name of Shpiro. As he was scanning the mailboxes, he came across the name Shpiro and knocked at the door. As the door opened, he asked the man if he was Shpiro and identified himself by the code phrase, "The sun is shining." The man immediately responded, "O, you don't want me, you want Mr. Shpiro the spy. He's on the 5th floor."

The young man jumped through many hoops in search of spy Shpiro, when in fact, all he had to do was to ask someone. Many times we make things difficult for ourselves instead of following a simpler process to accomplish the goal.

I remember a young man who had been hired by a national company for a salesman's job during the summer. All new recruits were asked to memorize a standard script to introduce themselves and their products. Upon meeting his first customer, the young man began his speech. He had barely started when the prospect immediately responded, "I'll take it." The young man looked surprised and shouted, "You can't take it yet. I have not given my full speech."

What if you had a misunderstanding with someone and as soon as you brought it up, he immediately responded, "I am sorry. I did not realize how I was coming across?" Would you continue to berate them and rub it in, even though your goal was already accomplished? Imagine asking a girl out for a date. As soon as you look at her and mention the word "prom" she says, "Yes!" Would you still continue your sob story, "Well, I am sorry I did not ask you earlier? I apologize that I asked your girlfriend first. I wish …" blah, blah, blah?

Imagine that you have just entered your kitchen to cook dinner and you receive a call from some relative to join them for a dinner to celebrate your aunt's birthday! Would you pout and gripe because it was a last-minute notice? Would you lick your wounds and scold them for not thinking of you earlier? Would you feel like you are not on their priority list? Or would you feel excited, thank them, join them and have a good time? You are not expected to give a gift. The host already knows that you were not informed in time to go to your favorite store to buy a gift. No matter how late the invitation, if you do not have any other obligation, be glad they thought of you, and go and have a great time. Don't make things complicated and ruin the occasion.   I remember some people almost having a coronary because they were not the first ones to be invited or given the news about their aunt Agetha's niece's husband's sister-in-law's cousin's granddaughter's engagement. Do you get it? Keep life simple!

Life is hard in itself; don't make it complicated. People should find you easy to reach, easy to teach, easy to do business with, easy to make friends with, and easy to work with. Don't expect others to be perfect. Take people at their word until they let you down. It will save you from playing the guessing game. Be real!

SOMETHING TO THINK ABOUT

Make a list of things you can do to simplify your life.

Never Say Yes and Never Say No!

NEVER SAY YES and never say no. "What kind of advice is that?" asked one of my associates when he read this. Let me explain it. Never say YES when your heart says NO. Similarly, never say NO when you believe that a YES vote will make a big difference and advance the cause of good. In other words, never endorse what you know is inconsistent with your inner conviction. Professor Jerry Harvey, formerly of George Town University is quoted in the program, The Abilene Paradox, "Collectively we endorse what we individually abhor." He points out that intelligent people who personally disagree with a course of action, enthusiastically vote in favor of it when they are in a group. People say yes when they actually mean no and they say no when they actually would prefer to say yes. This lack of integrity has infected corporate circles, city halls, halls of legislature, and even those who sit around our dinner table at home. We are just a bunch of gut-less slaves, walking around nodding our heads like robots and giving green signals to a train on its way to a wrecking yard. A wise teacher once advised, "Say yes when you mean yes and no when you mean no. Anything outside of this is a sign of a sick mind."

In The Abilene Paradox video, Professor Harvey shares a story. It seems that one Saturday night a boy walked into his office looking like a train-wreck. Professor Harvey inquired the reason for his poor disposition. "You would also look like me, professor, if you were getting married next

Sunday," stated the boy. "What's wrong with getting married?" asked the professor. The boy responded, "I am marrying the girl I don't like. We have nothing in common." "Well, why don't you call off the wedding?" asked the professor. "How can I call off the wedding? The cards are printed; relatives are already on their way. The girl's mother has a heart condition. If I call off the wedding, she'll keel over and her blood will be on my head," replied the boy.

No sooner had the boy left the office, than a girl walked in, who looked just as pathetic as the boy. Professor Harvey inquired the reason. "You would also look like me, professor, if you were getting married next Sunday," said the girl. "What's wrong with getting married," asked the professor. The girl responded, "I am marrying the boy I don't like. We have nothing in common." "Well, why don't you call off the wedding," asked the professor. "How can I call off the wedding? The cards are printed; relatives are already on their way. My mother has a heart condition. If I call off the wedding, she'll die and her blood will be on my head," replied the girl. Professor Harvey pointed out that the couple got married and checked into "Good Luck Motel" in Abilene, Texas. The Good Luck Motels enjoy 100% occupancy rate in our corporate circles.

People seem to be suffering from a disease called, "IDWTOA" – (I don't want to offend anyone). This is merely an excuse of an irresponsible person who lacks the resolve to make a decision. A person who lacks courage to stand for something falls for whatever blows in his direction. Imagine you are in a ship that is sinking in the middle of the ocean due to a decision made by a captain who is drunk. Would you simply hide in your corner? Never say NO when saying YES will save the ship. Also, never say YES when saying NO would help the ship reach its destination!

SOMETHING TO THINK ABOUT

Do you have the strength to say YES when you mean YES, and NO when you mean NO?

Live It Before You Give It!

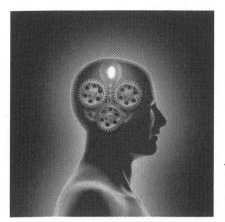

A STORY IS told of a woman who brought her young son to Mahatma Gandhi and asked the saint to advise the boy not to eat too much brown sugar because it was ruining his teeth. Mr. Gandhi requested the woman to bring the boy back in thirty days and he would counsel him. After thirty days, the mother brought the boy for counseling. Mr. Gandhi hugged the boy and asked him not to eat brown sugar because it was ruining his teeth. The boy immediately folded his hands like you do in prayer, bent down and touched Mr. Gandhi's feet (It is a sign of respect in India). Then he thanked Mr. Gandhi and promised that he would never touch brown sugar again. The woman was very unhappy with Mr. Gandhi. She stated that if that was all he was going to tell the boy, why did he not tell it thirty days ago? The great Saint responded that thirty days ago he too used to eat brown sugar and thus, he could not have advised the boy to give it up.

There is something about practicing it first before we advise others to embrace an idea. Years ago I was asked to participate in a youth conference to moderate a youth discussion group. The topic was "Staying Drug Free." There was a doctor who was very anxious to lead the group discussion. I politely gave him the opportunity to present his thoughts first. With great enthusiasm and an air of superiority he talked about the wisdom of remaining drug-free and the folly of giving in to peer pressure. Then came time for questions and answers. One of the boys asked the doctor if he was currently smoking or drinking. The doctor proudly declared that he was a smoker and drank, but only over the weekends.

Then he quickly asserted, "But as you can see, I am over twenty-one." A girl boldly voiced her opinion, "You are not only over twenty-one but you are also a hypocrite. You cannot be drugging yourself and asking us not to." Another boy asked me if I smoked and drank. I replied that I have never been attracted to smoking or drinking. I decided a long time ago that I will seek the help of friends who can help me stay drug-free. "Then you should be leading out in today's discussion instead of this doctor," a young man shouted.

That youth conference made such an impression on me that I have to examine myself whenever I speak in public or share my thoughts with people. The power of personal example is beyond compare. People can cast doubts on what you quote from books. They can discount your story about other people but when you share your personal experience there is no way anyone can refute it. There is something about living it before giving it. It adds credibility and builds respect and trust with your audience. Whether you are at home, at work or in the market place, there is no substitute for making sure that your deeds and creed match.

This world is full of people who think they have the license to tell others what to do but they are exempt from following the same principles. You often hear people say, "Do as I say and not as I do." This is one of the most useless phrases in our society. It institutionalizes hypocrisy. Be slow to promote what you personally don't wish to follow. Remember the old saying, "What you are speaks so loudly that I cannot hear what you say."

SOMETHING TO THINK ABOUT

When you speak in public, carefully examine yourself. You have no idea who is in your audience.

You may not be perfect, so admit that you are working on matching your deeds and creed.

A Firm Foundation for Greatness

AN INTERNATIONAL YOUTH organization, known as "Pathfinders," recently celebrated its 50th anniversary. This youth group has many similarities with another well-known organization, Boy Scouts of America. The program started with a color guard, flag salute and the Pledge of Allegiance. What impressed me the most was the Pathfinder's Law that was recited by all members who were awarded various medals for their academic excellence, community service and survival skills. The Pathfinder's Law has the following ten key pillars.

PURITY: I will be pure.

OBEDIENCE: I will be obedient.

TRUTH: I will be true.

KINDNESS: I will be kind.

RESPECTFULNESS: I will be respectful.

POSITIVE ATTITUDE: I will have a positive attitude.

HELPFULNESS: I will be helpful.

CHEERFULNESS: I will be cheerful.

THOUGHTFULNESS: I will be thoughtful.

REVERENCE: I will be reverent.

SOMETHING TO THINK ABOUT

With these principles as its foundation, what kind of a society would we create?

"Wanna-Be-Heroes"

O N THE JOURNEY of life, there are many "Wanna-Be-Heroes," who can hum the tune but they cannot stand straight on the dance floor. They can talk the talk but they cannot walk the walk. To make it to the finish line, you must become a person of character with a soft heart but a mind stronger than tungsten steel. Here is a test to measure your strength.

When the valley is deep and the mountain is steep,

When the desert-storm is raging and the heat is unbearable,

When the enemy is relentless, and you have no weapons,

When your misfortune is followed by more misfortune,

When the weather is turning from bad to worse
and a dense fog hides the path,

When your last penny is spent and the creditors
are knocking at your door,

When your feet are swollen and your hands
are too numb to hold the rope,

When you have exhausted all job leads, and
unemployment benefits are denied,

When your eyes are growing dim from
weeping and your eyelids are sore,

When your heart is sinking and the blood pressure is rising,

When you feel like you have been through the
mill and the worst is yet to come,

When your body is aching and you have the face to show it,

When you have been running all day but you haven't gained an inch,

When you have worked your fingers to the bone
but you have nothing to show for it,

When you feel tired like you have been around the
world but you haven't been anywhere,

When you feel like the day after the party but
you have not gotten out of bed,

When your mind makes promises that your body can't keep,

When your friends don't recognize you and the
neighbors think you're a stranger,

When you feel like giving up before even getting started, and

You can still count your blessings, you are a hero for all mankind.

SOMETHING TO THINK ABOUT

Read the obituary column in your local newspaper. If your name does not appear there, thank your lucky stars. You are a person with strength of character. The world needs you. Without people like you, this world would crumble like straw. You are on your way to a **better** land while others may be on a road to a **bitter** land.

Freeze the Termites Before They Bring Down Your House

T EAM MEMBERS WHO hold grudges, lose their temper easily, display rudeness, show lack of trust in colleagues, specialize in gossip, harbor an unforgiving spirit, don't say sorry when they hurt someone, cannot forget the unpleasant past, and have a hard time to start over when they fall are vicious termites. You must freeze their "buns" before they bring down your house. They are not friends who deserve to be tolerated, pampered, protected, consoled, cajoled or rewarded. You cannot control the damage by promoting them or by transferring them to another department. You cannot appease them by giving them a higher salary, larger office, bigger title or a designated parking space. You must put them on notice and if there is no significant change, you must show leadership and help them out – right out of the company, before they inflict irreparable harm to everyone. Here are some suggestions on how you may avoid turning into a termite yourself.

1.

Don't hold grudges

2.

Stay cool & hang loose

3.

Don't be rude or loud

4.

Build a Bank of Mutual Trust

5.

Avoid gossip – Have no favorites

6.

Forgive without being asked

7.

Be the first one to say sorry

8.

Learn the art of starting over

9.

Learn to bury it quickly

Lessons from the Chef

I AM NOT a good cook but I sure enjoy eating. Even though I don't eat anything that creeps, crawls, flies, bites, swims or talks back, I admire those who have a passion for the culinary art. I enjoy watching those who can cook, set an inviting table and make your mouth water just by the aroma. When I visit the Indian Tunduri restaurant or Benehana, it is a lot of fun to watch the chef, not just cook but also entertain. I have seen cooks burn their hands, set their hairs on fire, or spill boiling liquids trying to make food for the customers. On few occasions, I have let the toast stay in the toaster too long, I have let the milk boil until it bubbles over, and at times I have burnt the lentil dish so that it no longer was edible. Once I burnt my younger brother's mouth by putting the serving-spoon with boiling sugary liquid straight into his mouth right after I removed the pan from the fire. All these experiences have taught me some very important lessons.

When I was a child, my grandmother enjoyed my company. She often wanted me to help her in the kitchen. She was a good cook. She would often place a pot on the fire and ask me to watch it for her and not let it burn. Before rice cookers were invented, my grandmother cooked rice much better than any rice cooker I have ever seen. My grandmother had reduced rice cooking to a real science. She knew when to TURN THE FIRE UP and when to TURN THE FIRE DOWN. During my grandmother's time, there were no ovens, no timers, no cooking alarm clocks, no gas or electric ranges, and thus, no knobs to adjust the heat. Those were the days when you had to use your MIND and pay attention to what you were cooking. You could not put something on the fire and go shopping, watch your favorite soap opera, or go for a shower. You adjusted the heat either by putting more wood on the fire or by withdrawing some wood to lower the temperature.

Just by learning the art of applying the right amount of heat, we can create a delicious meal to entertain friends, guests or family. Our failure to adjust the heat to the desired level can ruin a good meal and invite unpleasant conversations around the dinner table.

If we can master the art of adjusting the temperature, we can do wonders for ourselves in managing our personal relationships with people. This principal holds true whether we are at home, at work or in the market place. Too much heat would burn the relationship. If the temperature is too low, it could simply keep things lukewarm. I remember, a young man who was dating a beautiful young lady. After two years of "blah" relationship, she threw in the towel, saying, "He has no direction or goal. He does not know where the relationship should go." By being aggressive, we can fade away the interest and drive away people. By being too low-key, we may give people the impression that we are likely to go to sleep on their dreams or put a wet blanket on their vision. Know when to be a shining star and when to just be the wind beneath someone's wings. From my grandmother I also learned that you cannot apply the same level of heat to all dishes. Some take low, some medium and some high temperature. Your have heard, "Different strokes for different folks." In order to bring out the best in people, know them and adjust to their temperament. The better we know people, the more equipped we would be in building bridges between ourselves and others. In our fast-paced society, we often take people for granted. Realign your mind. Invest time in people and build lasting relationships.

SOMETHING TO THINK ABOUT

Make a list of the people you have to deal with most of the time and evaluate your skills in applying the right level of heat to keep your flame lighted.

Treasure Life – It's Priceless

WHAT IS LIFE? What is the meaning of life? What is the purpose of life? Professors, philosophers, preachers and pundits for centuries have studied these questions. Books have been written, songs have been composed and poems have been recited in an attempt to explore the meaning of life. These questions have been of interest to me since I took philosophy courses during my graduate studies, and yet I have come no closer to fully arriving at answers to these questions. Life, its meaning and purpose differ significantly from individual to individual. However, here are my perspectives on life.

WHAT IS LIFE?

Life is love, live it.

Life is joy, share it.

Life is a gift, treasure it.

Life is patience, don't lose it.

Life is a mystery, discover it.

Life is fun, don't let it get boring.

Life is fragrance, let others enjoy it.

Life is bliss, taste it, you will like it!

Life is service, perform it cheerfully.

Life is music, don't forget the notes.

Life is laughter, laugh your heart out.

Life is sunshine, share it with the world.

Life is a challenge, meet it with courage.

Life is a dream, dream big and realize it.

Life is a rainbow, take time to admire it.

Life is now, don't wait until you get old.

Life is a promise, fulfill it, never break it.

Life is friendship, show yourself friendly.

Life is a mystery, invest time to unfold it.

Life is a story, crown it with a happy ending.

Life is a sport, don't just become a spectator.

Life is a journey, stay on course until the finish line.

Life is a song, sing it even if there is no one to clap.

SOMETHING TO THINK ABOUT

What do you think is the purpose of your life?

Aa

Strive To Be
Useful Always

O N FEBRUARY 5, 2005, Richard Bewes, the former rector of All Souls Church in London England, spoke at the Loma Linda University Church in Loma Linda California. His topic: "Be Useful." The wise and eloquent rector shared a story of his father who purchased a manual typewriter in the 1950's. He noted that.

Believe that you have what it takes to be useful. Unless we believe that we have something to contribute to our family, our community or our nation, we may go about our daily chores crying, complaining, pushing, pulling and sowing the seeds of discontentment. As long as you are breathing, you can be useful, and it begins by being useful to yourself. Start respecting yourself for the gifts you have rather than mourning over what you don't have.

Be willing to be useful. This world is full of talented people who, because of their unwillingness to participate in the life of the community, render themselves totally useless. They become parasites and infect the soul of the community with unproductive and useless pursuits. Be willing and the world will find plenty of use for your talents and skills. Once you begin to feel useful, your life will light up and you will become like an excited butterfly.

Be available. It is conceivable that one may believe that he is gifted and be willing to be useful, but unless he makes himself available, the world cannot benefit from his talents. Make yourself available. I once advised a talented young man to be useful to this planet. He quickly responded, "Right now I am focusing on providing for my family. When I believe I have enough for their future, then I will think of benefiting the world." Let me assure you that no matter how much you accumulate, you will always want more. Learn to live a lifestyle that allows you to care for your family and still spare a little to bless others. Don't wait until you have overabundance and plenty to spare for the needy; because you never will! Someone has well said that, *"We will never have enough of what we don't need to make us happy."* A selfish heart is like a bottomless pit; no one has ever been able to fill it. Like a goat, it is never satisfied. Like the desert, it can soak in all the rain and still be thirsty. Think about it!

Be willing to wait.   There are so many young and gifted people who are so aggressive to become useful that they push their way up the ladder before the world is ready for them. Thus, they are rejected and their inflated ego is decimated. Whenever you are anxious and you think the world is foolishly ignoring you, think of the letter "a". Waiting paid off big time! Today, no e-mail can go out unless it contains "@", letter "a" with a circle around it.

People like to be with those who make them feel important. Every human being wants to know if he/she is making a significant contribution in his/her corner of the world. Every husband, every wife, every son and daughter desires to know if their contribution to the family is making a difference. All big and bombastic tasks are accomplished by doing small and unnoticeable acts. Don't ignore the little favors. Gracefully acknowledge the contribution of others. At home, make the members of your family feel important. Affirm their positive contribution to the family. Thank them for adding value to the family unit. At the office, make your colleagues and supervisors feel that their help makes your work easier and more enjoyable. Offer to assist others and make their job easier. Don't just be a consumer and taker. Be a contributor and a giver. Giving is living.

SOMETHING TO THINK ABOUT

Inventory of your talents. Seek opportunities to be useful to others. Be accessible.

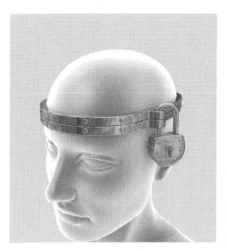

Avoid the Trap- "Everybody Does It"

IF I HAD received a penny every time I heard people proclaim, "Everybody does it," I could have been a millionaire. This is the first verse of a song sung by the people who postpone thinking before taking an action. When asked for the reason for their action, their usual response is, "Everybody does it." This is a trap that keeps people from thinking for themselves to safeguard their well-being. Here are a few reasons why you should not get trapped in this losers' game.

It is a myth. I have had the opportunity to speak before thousands of high school youth on the topic of drug addiction and smoking. Whenever I asked young people, "Why do you smoke?" "Everybody does it" was the most common answer. The fact of the matter is that only 22% of Americans smoke. Millions have quit. Everybody does not smoke. Most tobacco growers and cigarette manufacturers neither smoke nor drink. Everybody does not do it. It's a myth!

It is a lie. A myth is like a tradition that people have believed over the years regardless of the facts. A lie, on the other hand, is a statement you make as a fact, knowing that it is not. If you say, "Everybody does it," how do you know? Did you talk to everybody and ask them if they smoke or engage in a particular behavior? Learn to be truthful so the information you believe would be credible and a valid basis for your decision to stake your present and future on it.

It is harmful. Something in which everybody engages is usually not of value to everyone. Let's say that everybody tells a lie. Will that be a good reason for you to tell a lie? Will it build your character? If everybody were to drink and drive, will joining the crowd safeguard your well-being? If everybody spent more than they earned, will that give you a good reason to mortgage your future? Realign your mind. Take a stand. Don't follow the crowd.

It robs us of hope and a future. Trapped in the "Everybody does it philosophy," I was once confronted by my wise father. He put his two big hands on my shoulders, looked straight into my eyes and said, "Get it straight my boy, you are not everybody. You are my son and a member of the family that does not subscribe to such values. Don't ever sell yourself short and allow some loser to rob you of your hope for a brighter future. Now go on and be somebody special."

My father further advised me to follow the footsteps of the few who think before they speak; learn to give before they receive; allow others to impress them rather than burning people's ears with their monologues; calculate the cost before taking an action and who are guided by values that bless the people around them. This is how you heal your inner soul.

Don't despise the wise counsel of your mentors. It is by doing things we don't like to do that we achieve excellence in life. The average effort yields average results, gives birth to the average quality of life. An average person in America lives hand-to-mouth and would be in serious trouble if he misses two pay checks in a row. Be a cut above the average.

SOMETHING TO THINK ABOUT

Crowds are known to crucify innocent people. Discover what you are all about and be prepared to take a stand to defend it.

Travel Safely

MY BROTHER, JOHN, operates a Traffic School for violators. People who disregard safety rules, when given citations by law enforcement, come to his school to fulfill the education requirements imposed on them by the law. One day my brother took me to see one of the films they used at his school – "The Red Asphalt." The film taught me many important lessons for life. Let me share a few lessons with you. Each year, Americans drive over half a billion miles. The video recommended the following rules for ensuring safe travel:

Be courteous. Learn to manage risks.

Have a road map – be sure where you are going.

Make sure you are mentally and physically fit to travel.

Give yourself plenty of time to travel – don't be in a hurry.

Know the rules of the road – ignorance is not a valid excuse.

Give a complete physical to your vehicle before going on a long trip.

Make sure the brakes, windshield wipers and the horn are working properly.

Look ahead and keep your hands on the wheel at all times – be in control.

Make sure you can see the road – slow down when visibility is limited.

Warn the person behind you when intending to make a lane change.

Keep a safe distance between you and the driver ahead of you.

Look in the rear view mirror every five to six seconds.

Watch out for "blind spots" around your vehicle.

Watch for pedestrians and yield gracefully.

If in a collision, make detailed notes of the incident.

Never leave the scene of an accident - offer assistance.

Reduce speed in a construction zone or when the road is slippery.

Never resort to road rage, and no talking with your hands, please!

If you hit someone, stop, apologize, and exchange
information with the other party.

SOMETHING TO THINK ABOUT

Over 362,000 people are injured and thousands die on American highways each year. On the journey of life, the number of injuries inflicted by being careless and selfish are even more staggering. Just as we can prevent injuries and deaths on the highway by being courteous, we can ensure a safe passage for fellow travelers on their journey of life. The National Highway Safety Administration no longer uses the term "accident." Instead, they use the term "collision." It means that we have the power to act or react. We can choose to be safe or sorry!

Destiny is Paved by Choice

O UR MIND IS incredible. Consider it like a jar. You can pour crystal clear drinking water into it or you can pour liquid to unclog your sewer drain. You can store inspirational speeches of great leaders like Lincoln, Gandhi, Mother Teresa or you can store in it hateful doctrines of evil dictators. It all depends on your personal choice. You can choose to fly like eagles or you can shrivel up and give up on yourself. The story of two soldiers who returned from the Iraq War underscores the fact that our destiny is paved by our choices.

Iraqi POW Jessica Lynch came home to the United States to experience one of the most elaborate hero's welcoming-party this country has ever seen for a former prisoner of war. Her parents, neighbors, the city and the country bragged about her bravery and courage. Politicians invoked her name. Preachers pounded the pulpits as they praised the young woman for being a true American ambassador. No such heroic story ends without someone making a movie for posterity. The life of Jessica is immortalized by the movie, "Saving Private Jessica Lynch." Her fellow Americans lined up with eagerness just to shake her hand. She reminded us of the type of young men and women we would like to raise for the defense of the country and our collective honor. At a time when bullets were flying around her and her life was at stake, she made choices that would eventually result in making us all proud of her. The nation felt so proud of her, it felt like she was our modern statue of liberty with an eternal symbol of love for life and liberty for free people everywhere. Every father would love to have a daughter like Private Jessica Lynch.

The other soldier, Lynndie England made choices to participate in the Abu Ghraib prison scandal in Iraq that eventually became one of the world's most talked about shameful sagas, tarnishing the honor of the Untied States for decades to come. Newspapers and television reports around the world featured her shameful and despicable picture of holding the leash and dragging a naked prisoner in the hallway of the infamous prison. Instead of being praised and thanked for the tough life of a soldier fighting for the freedom of mankind, she was convicted of six of the seven charges against her and was given a three-year prison sentence. Choices! Choices! (Special Report, Time. May 17, 2004 and Associated Press, 9:08 p.m. ET Sept. 26, 2005).

People say that tough times build our character. Not so. When under fire, we reveal our character. Based on the choices we make, when hit by hard times, good people become better and bad people become bitter. The choices you make when no one is watching or when you have no one to tell you what to do, reveal your true self. Our destiny is paved by our choices. We carve our own destiny. How do you think you got where you stand at this moment in time? Not many realize that their future is being built by the choices they are making this very minute. Charting our future is not a mystery. It's like building a house; we can see the progress each day.

SOMETHING TO THINK ABOUT

Spend at least 15 minutes a day to reexamine the choices you made the day before.

Develop a profile of a person you want to become and see if your choices are leading you to your desired destination.

If You Sleep With a Skunk – You'll Smell Like One

A STORY IS told of a young man by the name of John Hanson. He was a fisherman. Once he brought home a load of herring. He cleaned them in his bathtub. The next morning his wife called him from her office all enraged, "John Hanson, did you clean the haring in the bathtub last night? I took a bath and now I smell like herring." The friends we keep; the music we listen to; the books we read, and the places we frequent for entertainment, all make an indelible impact on our lives. Consciously or unconsciously we tend to drift towards the likeness of the things and people we adore.

Realign your mind. Become a student of people. Some by their example will inspire you and make you feel you can fly or climb the highest mountain. Some will depress you and encourage you to go to your early gave. We all need someone to be the wind beneath our wings. However, we must choose our company wisely.

During my high school days, there was a boy whom I considered as one of my mentors. He was much older and always very kind and protective of my classmates and me. We admired him. I began to copy his mannerism. When in a group, I would watch his posture and stand as he would and position myself like him. Without being conscious of it, I began to adopt his way of speaking. During the summer holidays, when I arrived home, my mother noticed something strange about my mannerism. She did not want to embarrass me in front of others. However, one day when no one was around, she asked me why I was twisting my mouth to the left when I spoke. She asked me to look in the mirror and see how silly it looked. I immediately realized that I was copying my mentor and making a fool of myself.

On your journey of life, you are bound to encounter people from all walks of life. Some will seem to be very successful while compromising their values. Don't try to copy them even if they seem to be riding high at that time. Evaluate for yourself. Remember, their glory is temporary. Their peacock colors will fade away under the spotlight of truth. Don't fall for such vanity. Instead, you must seek friendship of people with substance and character. Encircle yourself with people who would gracefully help you make a "U-Turn" when you are on the wrong road and be your cheerleaders when you are on the right road.

If you are so particular about the clothes you wear, why not be just as selective about the friends you keep. Within your reach should be individuals who will love you even when you think you are unlovable; who will look you up even when you are playing hide and seek; and who will warm you up when you are like an iceberg. The people you hang around with are the mirror that reflects your inner makings.

SOMETHING TO THINK ABOUT

Carefully study your values, your work habits, your study habits and your organizational abilities and see if they are a reflection of the people around you, or are they a roadmap to your personal dreams and destination.

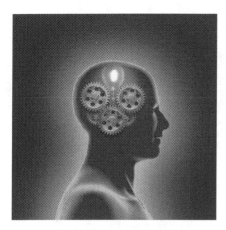

Realign Your Mind Pick Your Partners Wisely

IMAGINE THAT YOU are vacationing on your favorite resort island. It is a paradise! You are listening to your favorite music, sipping on your favorite beverage, and your favorite friend is running his/her fingers through your hair. You have a big grin like a cat that swallowed a canary. You are so excited to be alive. All of a sudden, the music is interrupted and you hear the President of the country announce, "War has started and we are not sure if anyone will survive." Then he directs you to a nearby bomb shelter and asks you to select a group of people you would like to save to repopulate the earth. Twenty people are standing at the door. You can select only ten in addition to yourself. Select the ten persons and place them in the space provided below.

CATEGORY A	CATEGORY B
A scientist	A gunman
A schoolteacher	A dishonest clerk
A PTA president	An uncaring mother
An army chaplain	A Selfish Union boss
A homeless shelter manager >>>>>>>>> <<<<<<<<<	An arrogant professor
A two-year old child	A hostile mechanic
A pregnant mother	A rude politician
An elderly mother	A selfish friend
A policeman	An angry sailor
A nurse	A rude nurse

1. _____   6. _____

2. _____   7._____

3. _____   8. _____

4. _____   9. _____

5. _____   10. _____

Take a look at your selection carefully. Did you select any person from Category B? Chances are you did not. Why? While the ten persons in category B may have the skills of persons in category A, they have an undesirable reputation. I have used these two lists many times. The persons in category B are rarely selected. If we had a choice to select the persons who will co-habit this earth with us, we would choose the ones with the best disposition and those who are likely to add value to our lives as they repopulate the earth. This should reveal to us that people in category B are not desirable. I strive to stay off of category B. How about you?   It is really sad but true that while many desire the company of caring and loving friends, they themselves remain toxic. Make it easier for people to live and work with you.

SOMETHING TO THINK ABOUT

Reasonable people do not appreciate the traits displayed in persons listed under category B. When Building a Better You, you are not eligible to wear any of those labels.

Realign Your Mind
Don't Have Fools
for Friends

A STORY IS told of a king who died and was succeeded by his son. Many elderly people from throughout his kingdom came to him and stated that his father had made their life miserable, and requested him to lighten their burden. The new king asked the people to come back in three days for his response.

The King summoned the elderly and wise consultants who had served his father and asked their opinion on the matter. They advised that if he would be a servant to the people and speak kindly to them, they would be his servants forever. However, the King rejected their advice and consulted his young friends who had grown up with him. His friends advised him to tell the delegates that "My little finger shall be thicker than my father's loins…My father chastised you with whips, but I will chastise you with scorpions" (The first book of Kings XII). The King addressed the delegation as advised by his foolish friends. People rebelled and half the kingdom succeeded and elected another king.

Everyone has friends. Some people have enemies disguised as friends. Study the word "friend." The last three letters of the word are "end." Thus, a friend is someone who knows all there is to know about you and still loves you until the end. It implies unquestionable loyalty.

When I was a child my father advised me to choose my friends wisely. Everyone is not worthy of the honorable title "friend." Before you call someone a "friend," ask yourself, am I prepared to be his friend to the end? Am I prepared to trust this person until the end? Am I prepared to expect the best, respect the best and accept only the best from this person? Am I prepared to always do my best for this person? I have taken my father's advice seriously. Over six decades of my life, I probably have five or six true friends for whom I am prepared to give my life, and even if someone were to sit on a hot grill to compromise my loyalty to them, I would not waiver. However, as friends, we do not gloss over one another's shortcomings. With genuine love, we correct one another and share ways to improve. The thought of ever hurting one another does not even cross our mind. We live thousands of miles apart and yet when we meet; it is as though we have never parted.

True friends bring healing to the bones. Bad friends rapidly grey your hairs and make you look old. They are a vexation to the soul. In our society, bonds of friendship seem to be paper-thin. Those who are married would recall the promise they made on the day of their wedding, "Until death do us part." Now, that's my concept of true friendship. Is it easy to find wise friends who will honor such a commitment? Hardly! In our culture, three out of five weddings never mature to becoming a marriage. Illness, economic hardship, social differences, pressure of rearing children, interference from in-laws and out-laws, competition with neighbors and selfishness do take toll. People throw in the towel and end their friendship over such frivolous and petty disagreements. So be wise and don't have fools for friends!

SOMETHING TO THINK ABOUT

When there are two wise friends, friendship will last to the end. If there is one wise friend and one foolish friend, their friendship has a chance to last to the end. However, the relationship of two fools will end abruptly or continue as a migraine headache. Be wise and don't sweat the small stuff. Learn to ignore some things, forgive some things, and constructively confront a few things.

True Friends

They are your second conscience.

They lift you up when you are down.

They are the wind beneath your wings.

They strengthen you when you are weak.

They want to feed not only your body but your soul.

They gloat with glory when your ship arrives in the harbor.

They never believe rumors about you even if told by angels.

They give you the glory and walk in your shadow occasionally.

They are prepared to stake their word to safeguard your integrity.

They will never give up on you even if you are down on yourself

They offer you their heart, not just big words and empty promises.

When there is only one life-jacket, they would rather give it to you.

They smack you right between your eyes to drag you back on track.

They would rather die than betray you and your confidence in them.

They never get tired of listening to your old stories and outdated jokes.

They weep when you are sad, and celebrate with you when you are glad.

They see you doing something approximately right and get excited for you.

If they were poor and you were rich, they pray that you would have even more.

When it is cloudy, dark, chilly and rainy, they embrace you like a warm blanket.

They are never afraid to step on your toes in order to keep you from going astray.

If there was just enough food to feed one person, they would rather feed you first.

If you were to lose a loved one, they will put their arms around you to reassure you.

They are prepared to care for your family if you were to kick the bucket prematurely.

If two of you were unemployed, they would give you the first shot at the available job.

If the road is long, narrow and steep, they would walk behind you to keep you from falling.

SOMETHING TO THINK ABOUT

A true friend is someone who knows all about you and still respects you and cares about you.

How many true friends do you have? How many of your friends think you are their true friend?

Enlarge Your Circle of Friends

There is no mountain we cannot climb,

no ocean we cannot cross and no battle that
we cannot win as long as we are blessed

with a circle of friends!

How large is your circle of friends?

What do you do to enlarge
your support network?

Be a Champion of Optimism

THIS WORLD IS infested with doomsday prophets. You can buy a dozen of them for a dime. They are enthusiastic, vocal, but their basket is full of thorns. If they are in sales, they blame their failure on bad weather, poor customers with bad credit, strict bank guidelines that make it difficult for customers to qualify, the owner's lack of advertising skills, the company's reputation in the community or their colleagues for being too aggressive to steal their deals. These negative gurus can spin yarns and even convince themselves that they are not responsible for their predicament. For troubles at the home front, they blame their spouse, their kids, their neighbors, their cat and God. I can write a book just on the blame game losers play.

Jimmy Sisneros, a salesman, shared an interesting story that sheds more light on the topic at hand. Two shoe salesmen were sent to a foreign country to explore business potential for their company. Upon reaching the new country, they noticed that hardly anyone wore shoes. Thus, one salesman wrote back, "There are no prospects for the shoe business in this land. No one wears shoes." The second salesman wrote back, "Wow! What an opportunity! No one has shoes. We will be able to sell lots of shoes." What is your perspective?

In developing an optimistic perspective on life and work, we cannot follow the crowd. The majority is seldom optimistic or right. If that were possible, 95% of Americans would not control just 3% of the country's wealth. The majority is always tuned to those who sing the blues.

Once an army general sent twelve of his men on a secret mission to case the land they intended to occupy. Ten men came back with bad news. They reported that the land was full of "giants" and we looked like ants in front of them. We don't stand a chance to take the land. However, two of the men returned with goods from the land. They reported that the land was very prosperous. The soil was wonderful for planting orchards. They showed the fruit they had brought to back up their optimistic forecast. The general believed the two disciples of optimism, raided the country and occupied without resistance.

Do you have some giants that are robbing you of your hopes and dreams? These giants come in many shapes and sizes. Here are a few examples of giants that obstruct our path to progress: Believing that we are no good, we have no skills, we are too old to develop new habits, we come from a poor family background, our parents had no resources to get us started in business, we do not have connections like others do, people don't like us, we don't get breaks like some do, our environment will never let us move upward, the company rules are not written in our favor, and so on. We beat up on ourselves so badly that when an opportunity looks at us, it is discouraged and moves on toward someone who will seize it, work it and take it to the bank. Disciples of pessimism look at themselves like the ten spies did. They were focusing on themselves rather than the opportunity at hand.

Our perspectives chart our course and pave our destiny. A wise man once said, "As a person thinks, so is he/she." Do you stare at impossibilities or at opportunities for a brighter future?

SOMETHING TO THINK ABOUT

Make a list of the "giants" that are robbing you of your dreams and take them down one by one.

Light a candle and burn the "giants." Identify three "hot" opportunities you want to pursue in the next three months.

Avoid Unproductive Pursuits like a Plague

I T IS DISAPPOINTING to see people with enormous potential feverishly preoccupied with unproductive pursuits. They close their minds to possibilities. Here are a few examples.

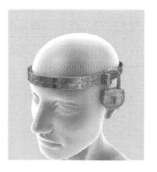

Laziness

Self-pity

Losing temper

Chasing the wind

Chasing the rainbow

Crying over spilt-milk

Chasing your own shadow

Wishing to relive yesterday

Trying to recover the lost time

Chasing after the lost opportunity

Trying to realize an aborted dream

Trying to call back ill-spoken words

Wishing you were single after being hitched

Taking comfort in your success of the days gone by

Wishing you were twenty-one after your 60th birthday

Wishing to be rich while spending more than you make

Looking for a second chance to make the first impression

Wishing to be known as an eagle while behaving like a turkey

Expecting a lion's share of benefits while not contributing squat

Hoping for a medal for reliability while failing to keep promises

Wishing to be a popular star while walking around like poison ivy

SOMETHING TO THINK ABOUT

Why do you think people keep looking for what they don't have instead of making something out of what they do have? Are you doing all you can to make the most of what you have?

Use Honey Instead of Vinegar

WHILE SERVING AS a human resource consultant to a corporation, one of my duties was to listen to employee complaints and offer assistance to resolve the problems. Once a young man came to see me with a complaint that the company did not recognize his expertise or reward him for his innovative ideas. Have you ever made a list of your accomplishments and how they add value to the bottom line of the company, I asked the young man.

It seems like the man was just waiting for a question like that. "I have left no stone unturned to let my immediate supervisor and the supervisor's boss know that I can do things ten times better than the company president's brother. I have often emphasized that I have far more knowledge than the owner's niece, but they have her in a position because she is a relative. They have the boss's sister managing one of the divisions which I can oversee with my eyes closed. The man, who is supposedly my supervisor, does not know half as much as I do. It appears that no one is interested in progress," said the man.

The man spoke with such enthusiasm about his greatness that if I were to believe him, I would also have to believe that the company was at the brink of disaster because of the fact that every position was occupied by an incompetent person. But I knew better!

I finally asked the man if he had made his feelings known to anyone! "Oh, YES. Everyone has been well advised about my skills and expertise. It's just that they all are burying their heads in the sand instead of giving me a break to take the company to the next level," added the man.

What do you think was this man's problem? He was wrapped in a triple blanket of self-conceit and riding so high in a hot air balloon that he was of no use to the company. He was blind. He could not see the giant wall he had built around himself that alienated everyone from him. He had rendered himself ineffective and incompetent to add any value to the company or contribute anything to the lives of people around him. He was concentrating in proving how incompetent others were that his own glaring follies were going unnoticed. He had become a poison oak that everyone avoided. The pill I recommended was difficult for him to swallow but he begrudgingly agreed to give it a try.

I suggested that he try to examine his own weak areas and overlook deficiencies of his colleagues and friends (I am not sure he had any friends). I further advised him to write thank you notes to his colleagues and commend them for the great work they do for the company. I asked him to start with the people he thought were the most incompetent and find at least two nice things about them and send them a note of appreciation. I have found this to be a miracle working strategy.

Be genuine and catch people doing something approximately right and praise them for it, and see them work their tail off to prove you right. Parents, employers, friends and leaders all resort to authority rather than grace and dexterity. People may comply with our demands out of fear or convenience but if we desire lasting results that would yield the expected fruit, we must be nice to people. People must feel good about us and around us. They must feel a bit taller than their actual size.

SOMETHING TO THINK ABOUT

What do you think of the saying, "If you can't say something nice, don't say it at all?"

The Best Is Yet To Come

MANY YEARS AGO, I heard a story of an elderly lady who played a very active role at her church. Whenever her friends needed help, she would be the first one to volunteer. In her church she was a leader when it came to organizing parties and potlucks. Everyone loved being around her. She was getting up in years and realized that she might not be able to continue her active role in serving her community. One day she made an appointment to see her pastor. She asked the pastor to help her write her will. In the will, she made a special request that when she dies, she wants her pastor to make sure that she would be buried with a fork in her hand. The pastor was puzzled. He finally asked her the reason for the fork. "Well, when I used to serve potlucks, I used to tell the people to keep their forks for the dessert. I want to remind them that the best is yet to come. There is a better world awaiting them after this one."

I have been deeply touched by this story. I think many of us miss out on the present by worrying and preparing for the future. We get wrapped up in guilt and sorrow for our past poor performance and fail to enjoy the blessings we do have. I have seen people wasting time by making repeated trips to the bathroom because they feel stressed out and a failure. Imagine the joy of going to bed with contentment and a positive attitude that the future is going to be even brighter. If you do your best and enjoy the present, you will have no fear of the future.

I was in my fifth grade and still did not know how to ride a bike. My uncle had bought a beautiful bicycle. He allowed me to learn how to ride the bike on his brand new machine. I had a hard time reaching the pedal. The first day I tried, I lost control and as I was attempting to get down, the front wheel of the bike went straight between an elderly lady's legs. She stood there ready to scold me. It was not a good day for me. Imagine if I had decided never to try bike riding again! We all go through life with challenges. However, most of us survive and do fairly well. Those who go through life with an attitude that "The best is yet to come," usually overcome their impediments and achieve their goals. Those who continually view every challenge as the end of the rainbow generally fulfill their expectations and perform poorly.

I grew up in a small village in India, surrounded by farms. The farmers faced many challenges. If it rained, it poured. When the rain let up, the drought made certain to make a visit. Then there were natural disasters like insect infestations that often ruined the crops. If the farmers did not have the attitude that "The best is yet to come," they would have abandoned their farms and starved their families and neighbors. Life is like a "merry go around." There will be ups and downs, but if your attitude is positive, you will experience more ups than downs. However, if your attitude is negative, you will have more downs than ups.

We often blame our misfortune on our spouses, neighbors, the boss or the circumstances. Blaming someone or something that we have no ability to change is an unproductive exercise. It is like feeding the horse that is not even in the race and expecting to win a medal.

For many, life would be a green pasture instead of a barren field if they would simply flip the switch and see the light. If they would simply adopt the elderly lady's attitude – "The best is yet to come."

SOMETHING TO THINK ABOUT

Do you go through life with a fork in your hand – imagining that the best is yet to come?

How can you make such an attitude contagious so others may see a rainbow in their life?

Expect Miracles

I BELIEVE THAT there is a "Great Spirit" (GS) that encircles the universe. It has eyes all over – nothing escapes its sight. It has ears all over – you cannot sigh without the GS fully experiencing it with you. No matter what you imagine, you are always a minute too late – the GS already knows about it. If you cry, the GS feels it and empathizes with you. If you rejoice, the GS smiles from ear to ear. When you are in the darkest valley of your life, the GS circles right above your head without your even realizing it. When you take off in the morning in your convertible speed demon, the GS already knows your destination. When your old jalopy gives up the ghost on the way to work, the GS is not surprised. If you have spent your last dime and there is no place to go, the GS seems to already know about it and is feeling the pinch with you. The GS knows your wants, your needs, your joys, your sorrows, your comings and your goings. I have no explanation for it. I have never seen the GS and neither has the GS ever directly confronted me. But I believe that there must be this GS that shows up unexpectedly to perform miracles to rescue us.

If you don't believe in the GS, then explain to me how a stranger happened to show up to help you fix a flat when you were stranded on a highway to nowhere? Explain to me how a swamp of millions of locusts would lick the crops of all the farmers around my dad's farm but leave our farm absolutely untouched? Explain to me how a missionary doctor would have traveled over three hundred miles in his jeep on an empty gas tank? Give me an explanation how I would get a letter from an unknown lady that read, "I understand you need $800 to register. Here is $500 and let your school know that I will be sending another $300 next month."

Do you suppose the GS had read my worried mind and communicated with the lady who was willing to listen and be an instrument of comfort to a needy boy? The GS knows that all humans are part of the same family, branches of the same tree and flowers of the same plant. We are here to help one another as we pass through this life.

I completed my 11th grade at the age of sixteen and embarked on a summer job to be a salesman for a national company. I was barely five feet tall and weighed 98 lbs. Realizing that my continued schooling depended on my coming back with a scholarship, I spent very little and saved every bit I made. Each day I went to a bank and sent a money order to the company head office. Someone had been watching me carrying cash to the bank. One day, while I was walking door-to-door, a big man commandeered me to a nearby park and handed me some white powder. "You are getting pale. You are going to die. You better take this medicine," said the stranger as he demanded that I hand over to him cash for his generosity to look out for my health. I was scared. I tried to stall the conversation but the man became intense. All of a sudden I saw two women walking toward where we sat. As they came near us, I quickly handed Rs.10 ($3 at that time), and the man took off. I turned around to thank the women for saving my life, but there were no women. I had the white powder tested. It was poison.

Do you suppose the GS was circling right over the scene to ensure that I would be alive to write this? Expect miracles. You have probably gone through many experiences that have no explanation. Behind every face you see a miraculous story. Our expectations are like self-fulfilling prophecies. Whatever you expect usually becomes a reality.

SOMETHING TO THINK ABOUT

There are millions of true-life experiences just like the ones described above. I hope you believe in miracles. I do!

Mend It or End It Before It Cuts Your Life Short

PARADIGM MEDICAL MANAGEMENT Company, a California--based health care organization, specializes in advanced wound healing medical modalities. The majority of the clients are diabetics with chronic wounds. The Company operates many Wound Care Centers. If left untreated, these chronic wounds can lead to amputations and cut short a person's life abruptly. These chronic wounds compromise one's life, health and happiness. A large number of these chronic wounds are diabetes related.

In the case of juvenile diabetes, the illness is a cause of compromised health status during childhood when an early infection retarded the body's ability to produce insulin. However, the adult-onset diabetes is primarily related to one's lifestyle. The body begins to produce too much insulin that is not regulated properly. The good news is that nearly 80% of the adult-onset diabetes is controllable, and in many cases even the medication can be eliminated by improving one's lifestyle. However, what amazes me is the fact that not many are willing to listen to, or adhere to a lifestyle prescription until their back is up against the wall and they begin to stare at amputation, blindness and non-healing chronic sores and wounds. Instead of changing their way of living, many simply adjust to a compromised quality of life. How sad!

I have often wondered why humans who are gifted with an amazing power to think, choose and change do not exercise their abilities to improve the quality of their lives! Hardly a day goes by when someone does not tell me about some chronic condition that is compromising his/her happiness and cutting his/her life shorter and shorter each day. Here are a few suggestions to end old and harmful habits and mend your ways to improve the quality of your life.

- If your job is driving you insane, get a life, love it or leave it.

- If your relationship with someone is oozing with pain, end it or mend it.

- If you use plastic money and you are drowning in debt, get help before it gets hopeless.

- If you are allergic to people but your job demands public contact, get with it or out of it.

- If you look pleasantly plump and you are left off the social list, get fit or quit complaining.

- If you live with your relatives or friends and you don't like how they treat you, get your own place, or start respecting them and their feelings.

- If you owe a relative or a friend and they begin to quack about it to embarrass you, pay them back or develop a thick skin or slippery feathers like ducks.

- If you cannot contain all your chicken in the little chicken-coup you have, build a bigger chicken-coupe or set the chicken free.

SOMETHING TO THINK ABOUT

You don't have to live with what you don't like. You don't have to put up with what you can change. You don't have to settle for it if you have the courage to get a better deal. It's all in your hands. There are no short cuts on the road to success. If you don't like something, end it or mend it.

Get a Life — Use Commonsense

- You cannot CUSS the chef and expect to be served filet mignon.

- You cannot despise the children and expect the parents to invite you for dinner.

- You cannot stop payment on your check and expect the merchant to extend more credit to you.

- You cannot plant poison ivy in your neighbor's yard and expect him to plant roses in your garden.

- You cannot drill holes in the bottom of the ship in which you are traveling and then be surprised when tossed into the ocean to swim with sharks.

- You cannot walk around like the boat has sunk and expect people around you to think that you were their "manna" for motivation.

- You cannot fly around like a stinging bee and expect people to roll the red carpet in your honor and worship the ground you walk on.

- You cannot behave like a Sherman tank and expect people to welcome you with a smile.

- You cannot keep dishing dirt to others and expect to win the "Award for Congeniality."

- If you get worn out walking with children at a picnic, you will not be able to keep pace with the soldiers on a mission.

- If you walk around carrying a two-edged sword, don't expect to win a Nobel Peace Prize.

- You cannot be a member of a MAJOR League while playing in a MINOR League.

- If you would not do more than what you are paid for, don't expect the company to pay you for more than what you do.

- If you are waiting for fair weather to plant, at harvest time you can expect weeping instead of reaping.

- Your Grandma was right! "You attract more bees with honey than with vinegar."

- Treat your body better than you treat your car, because spare parts for your body are not only expensive but also hard to find.

- Your fingerprints are rare, one in a billion match. Be selective on what you place your thumbprint.

- Your name represents everything you have become thus far. Be very selective when you attach your name to something or someone.

- You cannot be a winner as long as you are bent on making others feel like losers.

- If you would spend half as much energy on improving yourself as you spend in changing the world to suit you, your world would be much better than you think it is.

- Don't be allergic to commonsense; it is free and it saves lives. Commonsense may be beyond the reach of the rich, the famous and the powerful, but it's a friend of the wise.

SOMETHING TO THINK ABOUT

Think about the time when using commonsense saved you from embarrassment.

HOW IS COMMONSENSE RELATED TO WISDOM?

_____

_____

_____

_____

_____

_____

_____

_____

_____

_____

_____

_____

_____

_____

_____

_____

_____

_____

_____

_____

_____

_____

Build to Last

MANY YEARS AGO I learned an ancient story. A king told his Prime Minister that he had a very special friend whom he wanted to honor. "What would you like to do for him?" asked the Prime Minister. "I was hoping that you would build me a very large and special palace that I would give to my friend," said the king. He put the prime minister in charge of the construction and gave orders to his finance minister that whatever the prime minister needed must be provided to him.

The prime minister accepted the assignment, but in his heart he felt betrayed by the king. "I have been his faithful friend for many years. He has never offered to build me even a house, and here he is asking me to build a big palace for some friend." He called his contractor and told him that he wanted the palace to look pretty from the outside, but he did not want to waste all the money on some unknown friend of the king. He ordered the construction crew to spend only half the allocated amount on the palace.

Finally, the palace was completed. He requested the king to take a tour of the palace. The king saw that the palace looked very pretty. He summoned his noble guests and bragged about the friend whom he wanted to honor for his loyalty and dedicated service to the kingdom. "Now you must be wondering who that special friend is. Let me introduce him to you. He is none other than my prime minister who has served me and the kingdom with dignity and pride," said the king. Then the king handed the key to the palace to his prime minister. How the prime minister wished he had built the palace so it would last!

This story has been a guiding light for me over the years. Whatever I build, I try to build it to last – who knows I may have to live in it. I think about the outcome before I make my decisions because I know I have to live with the consequences. We live in a "Throw away" culture. Whether it's the goods and services or the relationships, it just seems like we don't build to last. Most Americans prefer foreign-made automobiles. How many American-made automobiles carry 100,000 miles warranty? Not many. Take a look at your television, plasma screen, microwave, shoes, cameras, cell phones and telephones. I could go on an on. Of course things can be built cheaper oversees but more than that, they are built to last and capture the American market. You are an architect. Always build to last. It carries your name!

However, of greater interest to me is how we build relationships and interpersonal networks. Do we invest time to build to last? Think of the last time you wished good morning to a co-worker did you wait to hear his/her response? What about the time when you asked your neighbor "How are you?" Did you give him the chance to tell you that he was out of work, his health insurance had run out, his children had to quit school because they don't have transportation, their refrigerator has been on the blink for weeks and they cannot store any food in it, they are behind in their mortgage payment and have no food for dinner. What about the time when you were watching your favorite show, "Simpson's," "Days of Our Wives," or "As the Stomach Turns," and your child wanted to talk to you? Did you turn off the tube? I doubt it! What excuse did you make when your sister invited you to go to the movie with her? We invest very little and expect things to last forever – that's a pipe-dream. Take time and build to last or you will regret later.

SOMETHING TO THINK ABOUT

Build it so well that you would enjoy it immensely if you were to inherit it. When you lend your name or place your fingerprints on something, take personal pride. Don't be in a hurry. Don't resort to shortcuts. Do the right thing, not what is convenient. Do what will bless others also, not just benefit you. Do good to others with empathy, not just to look good in public. Slow down and think things through. Pause and consider the impact of your actions. What if this was your only chance to make a lasting impression! What if this was your only opportunity to give someone a ray of hope? Don't rush it!

So Many Weddings-
So Few Marriages

A WEDDING IS a global ceremony that affords every person who wants to get hitched the opportunity to be a hero for a moment, make a movie and in some cases, drown himself in debt. In many countries, the parents of the girl beg and borrow to give to the parents of the prospective groom "dowry" they cannot afford. The richer the parents of the groom, the more hungry they seem to be to sell their son to the parents of some poor girl to be her bright and shining star.

In the United States, the couple scripts every detail of every move, and many borrow money to have a wedding. They invite a large number of guests, even those they don't like and cannot afford to feed, rent fancy clothes they would never wear again, and exhaust themselves under distress they try to hide.

A wedding is an event, while a marriage is a journey. Wedding can be a make-believe ceremony while a marriage demands naked truth and humility to get real and stick together "for better or worse." A wedding is not a true snap-shot of a marriage. Consider how unreal a wedding ceremony is — a man dresses up in a rented tuxedo and a woman takes a long walk in a church. (most of them will never be seen in a church until they are given their last rights) dressed up in a thirty-foot long veil, while children scatter rose petals in her path. Imagine a cast of men and women dressed up as groom's men and bride's maids. How many maids can the couple afford after the wedding? In the presence of hundreds of guests, man and woman pledge allegiance to each other to be faithful until they breathe their last. This promise is made with euphoric-feelings imbedded in a make-believe ceremony. Nearly 51% of those who make a commitment, "until death do us part," recant their promise like the new-year resolution made by "wanna-be-thin" people.

So many weddings and so few marriages! In fact, there are more second marriages in America than first-time marriages. If this trend continues, one day we may all be related as one big family. Can there be a marriage after the wedding? Let me share a few tips on how to turn a wedding into a lasting marriage.

- Write down ten things that gripped your heart and prompted you to say "1 Do" and keep the list   in a safe place.

- Once a week, repeat at least one activity that brought you joy before marriage.

- When things get tough and you have second thoughts about your marriage, take out the list of things that prompted you to say "I Do," and rekindle the fire.

- When you are unable to bear the burden alone, seek help in time and protect your investment. Nothing is more important than your marriage; not money, not your job, not all the oil in Saudi Arabia, or the presidency of the universe. Accept your own weaknesses and forgive others without being asked. Marriage usually fails when we take each other for granted and fail to communicate.

Don't let outsiders interfere in your marriage. Don't believe hear-say. Learn to keep your mind's hard-drive clear. Be not just a spouse but the best friend. Let self take back seat in the best interest of the overall good of the family. Seek opportunity to praise your partner at lest twice a day and go on a date at least once a week. Look in the mirror as often as you can, especially if you intend to wipe the dirt off of your partner's face. Be the wind beneath your partner's wings.

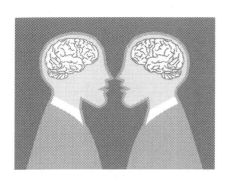

So Many Boys, So Few Men – So Many Girls, So Few Women

SEVERAL YEARS AGO, I saw a bumper sticker on a car that read, "So Many Boys, So Few Men, So Many Girls, So Few Women." I am not fully sure what the owner of the vehicle meant by it, but I believe it implies a lack of maturity. It refers to a stage of development in life rather than to one's chronological age. It means that the adolescent stage has extended far beyond what is considered to be a normal cycle of growth. It means that the individual has not yet graduated to a stage where he/she is capable of taking personal responsibility for his/her actions. Let me share a few tips on how to differentiate men from boys, and women from girls. Real men and women:

- live by their word and keep their promises;
- have positive values and strong loyalty to their family;
- are not wheel-barrows, you don't have to push them to action;
- never abandon the kitchen because the temperature is too high;
- are not mules; you don't have to use a 2x4 to get their attention;
- are people builders and masters of the art of diplomacy and tact;
- create win-win transactions in life and live by a sense of fairness;

- are not horse-carts, you don't have to pull them to move forward;

- are proactive, have a goal with a deadline and passion for excellence;

- are persistent, resilient, and know how to start over if they should fall;

- are not a starfish, they don't close up after a brush with outside forces;

- accept counsel gracefully and do not fall apart when corrected by others;

- are self-directed and do not wait for someone else to light a fire under them;

- know how to listen, how to cry, how to laugh and how to live a balanced life;

- when things go awry, they examine themselves rather than blaming the world; and

- have virtuous attributes: courage, humility, modesty, integrity, honesty and hard work.

Many resort to silent treatment to express their displeasure with their partner. This is one of the worst ways to resolve a conflict. If the marriage was rocky before, silent treatment would certainly make the cord snap. Many blame the partner when things go wrong. The blame game would add little to the solution but it will surely seal the ill fate of a relationship. Thus, take responsibility. Mend what you can and end what you cannot live with.

SOMETHING TO THINK ABOUT

When you are all by yourself, take a good look in the mirror and assess your life.

Are you content being the person you see in the mirror?

What suggestions would you give to the person in the mirror to achieve excellence?

SUGGESTIONS TO THE MAN IN THE MIRROR

_____

_____

_____

_____

_____

_____

_____

_____

_____

_____

_____

_____

_____

_____

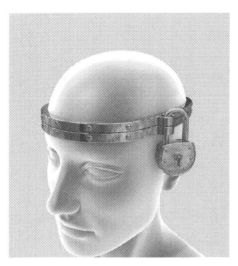

Listen With an Open Mind (Part I)

I F YOU COULD hide in a closet and hear what your friends fight over in their homes, you would hear them repeating like a broken record, "You just don't listen to me." People love to talk, and mostly about themselves and their great feats, but listening to others is an art that is rapidly vanishing. Listening is loving. Listeners make better lovers, better workers, better supervisors, better leaders, better friends and better neighbors. Our listening skills provide others the opportunity to teach us. We don't learn anything when we are speaking. We learn only when we are listening. That is probably the reason why we have two ears and only one tongue. Ears are placed outside the body while the tongue is placed behind two gates – the first gate can cut it off, and the second gate can seal it off. And yet, it is the tongue that gets out of control. Imagine if the tongue was actually hanging outside the mouth, it would create ten times more trouble than it does now! Our ability to listen signals our hunger for learning, improving and developing higher levels of problem-solving skills. It is said that even a fool is considered wise when he is silent. At your office meetings, become a super listener and everyone will declare you a wise person. They will seek your counsel. Here are a few tips to help you enhance your listening skills.

Listen With Your Heart: Show genuine interest in the speaker and find out what is important to your listener. Pay full attention and seek to understand the other person's point of view.

Cut Out Distractions: It is rude and shows lack of respect to answer your telephone, cell phone or write notes to others while someone is trying to speak with you and express their concern. No matter how small the issue, you must listen with your heart. What seems trivial to you may be keeping the other person awake at night. Pay attention!

Give Active Listening: Sit straight and look at the person. Occasionally ask questions and seek clarification. It tells the other person that you are listening and paying attention.

Don't Interrupt: Allow the other person to speak. Don't interrupt or complete their sentences. It is a sign of impatience and shows lack of respect for the other person.

Listen to Learn-Not to Argue: The purpose of listening is to receive enough information so you may be able to resolve a problem or work on a project constructively. It is not the time to contradict and condemn the other person or his/her viewpoints.

You May Disagree But Remain Agreeable: Even if you don't fully agree with the other person, you must respect their perspective so they may respect yours. It is alright to disagree and share different perspectives. Newer and more innovative ideas are born in healthy disagreements.

Listen With an Outcome in Mind: Never lose sight of the end result you expect from your transaction. The purpose of listening is to understand the other person and use the information to build a bridge that would allow both parties to walk together to the land of mutual understanding.

SOMETHING TO THINK ABOUT

Find a mentor who is a good listener and learn from his/her listening skills.

Make a list of 10 things you can do to become a better listener. Practice your listening skills when you are with people. Speak less, speak in a low tone, and speak slowly and clearly.

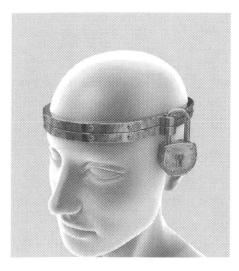

Listen With an Open Mind (Part II)

L ISTENING IS AN art. However, since most people enjoy talking more, listening is rapidly becoming a less attractive art. People love to talk about themselves and their accomplishments. For many, listening to themselves is the sweetest sound to their itchy ears. To be a good listener, one has to keep his mouth shut and ears wide open, and this for some is harder than climbing Mount Everest. It requires one to focus on understanding the other person's viewpoint instead of pushing his/her own. Here are some more tips on becoming a better listener.

Be a Focused Listener: Most people just want to be heard. They want someone to give them attention. They want to know that what they have to say does matter to someone. Give your full attention. Try to understand what is being said and why. Failure to be an attentive listener will deprive you the golden opportunity to get accurate information that may help you resolve the problem.

Don't Quibble Over Words – Get The Message: When an overweight person says, "I know you don't want a fat person on your team," he is not playing a psychic and giving you a printout of your mind. He is expressing his feelings of anticipated rejection. You don't have to be defensive, thinking that the person is attacking your value system. This is your opportunity to build him up and relieve his fears of being ostracized due to his weight. When your spouse says, "I know I don't rank high enough on your schedule," it is not a statement of affirmation of your daily planner. She is hanging up a billboard in front of you with a message, "Quit neglecting me." Words are simply the symbols people use to hide their inner thoughts. A good communicator knows how to read the smoke signals.

Don't Guess. Here is a sentence that has almost seven different meanings. What do you understand by the following sentence? "I DID NOT SAY THAT PAUL STOLE THE COOKIE OUT OF THE COOKIE JAR."

1. Are you saying that Paul did not steal the cookie out of the cookie jar?

2. Are you saying that it was not Paul who stole the cookie out of the cookie jar?

3. Are you saying that you did not verbalize that Paul stole the cookie out of the cookie jar?

4. Are you saying that it was not this cookie that Paul stole out of the cookie jar?

5. Are you saying that the cookie was not stolen from inside the cookie jar?

6. Are you saying that it was not the cookie jar from where the cookie was stolen?

7. Are you saying that it was not the cookie that was stolen?

It is always better to seek clarification rather than guessing and defending the wrong message, or responding to a question that no one has raised. Listen to learn. Listening is loving and good listeners make better lovers. The better you listen, the more you are loved by those around you.

SOMETHING TO THINK ABOUT

Are you a good communicator? Do you read the smoke signals? Make a list of mistakes made by poor listeners and work systematically to improve your listening skills.

Avoid Information Overload

A STORY IS told of a preacher who moved into a new town. The first week he was to preach, it snowed heavily. When time for church service came, there was only one person in the entire church. The preacher asked the man if it would be alright for him to preach even though there was no one else to hear him. The man replied, "Well, I don't know much about preaching, I am a farmer, but if it was feeding time and only one cow showed up, I certainly would go right ahead and feed her." The preacher considered it a green light to deliver his message. Forty-five minutes into the speech he had barely touched the fringes of salvation. He continued for another thirty minutes. When he concluded his sermon, he asked for the man's reaction. The man responded, "Well, as I said, I am a farmer. I don't know much about preaching, but if it was feeding time and only one cow came in, I would certainly feed her, but I would be doggone if I would feed her the whole load."

One of the most common problems in communication is that we try to overload the listener. By sharing too much information, even though we may not verbalize it, we signal unrealistic expectations and thus, overwhelm and frighten our listeners. Here are four simple suggestions to help you prevent information-overload and retain the attention of your audience.

Know Your Audience. Don't speak over their heads. The news media tailors their message to fifth or sixth grade level. Speak shorter sentences. Include just one thought in each sentence. Tailor your message so the least educated person would be able to understand it. Don't try to impress your audience. The purpose is to get your point across, not to convince them that you have a Ph.D. Remember, it's easier to chew and swallow smaller bites.

Don't share too much at one time. People have a short attention span. They cannot digest too much at one time. Television may be partly responsible for distorting people's attention span. In the 1950's, the television scene used to change every three and one-half seconds. In the 1960's, the time was reduced to three seconds, in the 1970's, the time was reduced to almost two seconds. Today, when you watch television, you will note that every second or two, new things are being added to the story. People cannot concentrate on one subject for more than a few seconds.

Use smaller bites to feed your audience. Break down the large body of material into smaller chunks and adopt the appropriate method to convey it to your audience. As in the case of some diabetics or hypoglycemics, it would be better to feed them several small meals than one big one.

Cater to your listener's senses. Some people are more visual and some are better in comprehending abstract thoughts. Every type of fish requires different bait. In our culture, reading is almost going out of style. We have to employ more video and audio means to convey our message. Use as few words as possible to convey your message.

Conduct a reality check. Ask for your listeners' feedback to ensure that you did not simply waste your breath. Never assume that your audience got the message.

SOMETHING TO THINK ABOUT

If your message does not get through, don't blame the audience. Examine yourself and improve.

Learn to Live Longer Now

1.

Have a minimum of 7-8 hours of sleep daily. Body needs at least 6 -7 hours to repair itself and rejuvenate.

2.

Walk at least 30 minutes a day (two miles). Exercise releases endorphins – body's natural hormones to get you high on life.

3.

Eat breakfast regularly. Have a good lunch and light supper before 7 p.m. Clean your body. Eat fruits and vegetables. No snacks. Snacking is like putting a second load in the washing machine while the first is still churning.

4.

Minimize eating things that creep, crawl, fly, bite, swim or talk back. Reduce animal products. If you must eat meat, use fish, chicken or turkey.

5.

Don't take things personally. Be friendly. Develop a sense of humor. Forgive without being asked. Keep the load off your back. Learn to laugh at yourself. Be happy. No one enjoys being around a grouch.

6.

Drink at least 7-8 glasses of water daily. Avoid the use of alcohol or soft drinks. Don't use tobacco. Tobacco causes heart disease, cancer, high blood pressure, gets you tired, and causes wrinkles.

7.

Stay away from sweets – have fruits for deserts. Sweets reduce the body's natural immune system to fight colds and other illnesses. Sweets increase your risk for diabetes and many other health problems.

8.

Listen more. Speak less (in a low tone of voice) and don't get angry. Anger leads to danger

(D+ ANGER). Don't discuss family problems after 8:00 p.m.

9.

Take a trip to paradise daily. Take fifteen minutes in the morning and evening and sit quietly on the floor with your hands in your lap. Think of all the good things that have happened to you since you were a child. Turn off the negative tapes – think only positive thoughts. We are surrounded by negative elements and noises that create stress and emotional discomfort. We need to develop an environment that would induce peace and tranquility.

10.

Spend less than you make. Focus on your needs instead of your wants. After the basic needs are met, money does not add to happiness. In fact, it may add more unhappiness. Live a balanced life. Pray and God will help you stick to this plan!

SOMETHING TO THINK ABOUT

Strive to live well instead of just making money and acquiring things. Stay healthy. All the money in the world cannot buy back your health.

All Work and No Play – Is the Formula for Making a Dull Boy!

YEARS AGO READER'S Digest credited Ned Parker, quoted by Alex Thien in Milwaukee Sentinel, with the following story:

A man was marooned on an island for months. One day, as he scanned the horizon in search of a ship, a skin diver in a wet suit came out of the water. The man stood there astonished as the diver pulled off the headgear, and a mane of golden hair fell to her shoulders. "Wow!" said the man. The skin diver smiled and said, "Is there anything I can do for you?" "Well," replied the man, "I haven't had a martini for a year, but I don't suppose you could get me one." She smiled again, unzipped a side pocket on her wet suit, took out a flask and poured him a perfect martini. "Something else?" she asked. "I'd give anything for a good cigar." The diver quickly opened another pocket, pulled out a cigar and lit it for him. "Anything else?" she asked. "Nope. I'm just fine now." "You mean you don't want to play around after being here all alone for a year?" The man's eyes lit up. "Say," he said, "don't tell me you've got a set of golf clubs in there too!"

As the old saying goes, "All work and no play is the formula to make a dull boy." Most major corporations these days have physical fitness facilities for their employees. Companies with wellness promotion programs report significant savings in employee health-related costs. Workers who exercise regularly, eat a balanced diet, maintain their ideal weight, refrain from smoking and drinking seem to take fewer sick days than their counterparts who have poor health practices. Also, employees who spend time with their families and friends and have a better social life, seem to be happier, and, are sick less often than those who are loners.

When I worked for the government, I operated an employee wellness program for eleven years. Once I gave an assignment to the group to spend at least half a day each month around a body of large water or in the woods as a family in order to renew their batteries and reduce their day-to-day stress. Two weeks later I was at Costa Mesa Beach in California, ready to take my family for a boat ride. After parking my car I was walking toward the marina. A booming voice called "Dr. Massey." I paid no attention, thinking that there must be another person by that name. The voice called again and this time called me by my first name. I realized that there is someone who really knows me. As I turned around, it was a person from my employee health program. He told me that he had not been attending the program because the assignment I had given about spending a half-day around some large body of water had taken care of their stress and they did not feel the need of my program any more. They were spending time together as a family, having fun, improving their communication with one another, and feeling better about their life and relationships.

Balance your life between work, family, building personal health, community service and your hobbies. If you are not having fun, then your life is in the negative zone. You must first like yourself enough to take care of yourself before you can help pull others out of their misery-land. It is amazing how much leisure time can be found by getting ourselves organized. If we are not organized, we have to work harder and it takes longer to accomplish simple tasks.

SOMETHING TO THINK ABOUT

In the eastern culture, life in balance means good health. If life is not in balance, one is sick.

Wake Up in the Arms of Joy Every Morning

CAUTION: BELIEVING AND acting on the suggestions in this chapter may be hazardous to your old and traditional ways of thinking and living. It may totally ruin your plans for mourning, groaning, complaining, pouting and all other outbursts of lame excuses about how you ended up in life where you did not expect. This article is meant to rob you of your urge to blame others when life deals you a raw hand and deprives you of JOY, pure joy!

Life is a JOYFUL experience. If you don't believe it, imagine the fun dead people have! Without JOY, life will lose its luster, its meaning and its very purpose. The suggestions contained here have been known to ignite a burning desire to expect and respect only the best from yourself and others. You have been on your journey of life for years; why not pursue the path that will add joy to the world around you, and, most of all, to your inner soul. So, go ahead, read it, enjoy it, live it, give it and make my day, and yours!

Wake Up in the Arms of Joy Every Morning. Every day, when I get up in the morning, I read the obituary section. If I am alive and kicking, every other challenge from then on seems like a downhill run. I wake up in the morning at 5:15 a.m. and get on the road by 5:30 for a 45-minute run. Just to feel the fresh air entering the lungs gives me reassurance that it's going to be a fantastic day. I look up to the sky and see the stars, and sometimes even a full moon. It is so inspiring to greet the universe and welcome the day. My very existence is a sign that there must be a purpose for living. I cogitate on my life, my mission, my vision and my action plan for the day. I review the potential challenges and opportunities to make a difference. By 6:15 a.m. I complete my exercise routine and spend some time in meditation. By 7:00 a.m. I leave for the office to add value to someone or something. I leave my office by 8:30 p.m. with no regrets. How was your day today?

When you open your eyes in the morning, be happy that you were not one of the millions of people who died last night. Be glad that you were not one of the many who checked themselves into hospitals, emergency rooms and intensive care facilities. Additionally, there are millions of people who have no eyesight to see this beautiful day, and many more who have eyesight but no vision. Take three deep breaths and say WOW! I am glad to be alive. It's going to be a great day! Be on a mission. To brighten your own day make at least two people happy today. As you wake up in the morning, imagine that you have just come back to life. All the disappointment, rejections, hurts, bruises, shortcomings, negative songs, poverty-prone thinking, political wrangling, and interpersonal squabbles were all buried with you last night and now you are a brand new person. You have a new lease on life. You can now operate on all sixteen cylinders. Go for it!

SOMETHING TO THINK ABOUT

If you could begin your life all over, what changes would you make in the way you think, the way you utilize your time and the way you take responsibility for your life and work?

Jump for Joy Daily

I F IT IS worth starting the day, it is worth starting it with a smile on your face and with your favorite exercise. My favorite exercise is jogging. It releases endorphins that literally get you high on life naturally. When you start the day with exercise, you feel good; look good and think better all day. It calms your nerves, gives your skin a healthy glow, makes your face radiant and builds your immunity to defend you against all those germs waiting to feast on you. Exercise prevents a host of cardiovascular diseases such as heart disease, diabetes and hypertension. Exercise prolongs youth and delays aging. It reduces stress and equips you to build a bridge to cross over your troubled waters all day. Here are a few commonsense principles to keep in mind when you start an exercise program:

Be Positive: If you hate to walk, jog or move your muscles, you will increase your blood pressure while exercising. It is important that you have a positive attitude and appreciate the value of exercise in order to benefit from it.

Get Enough Sleep: The body needs 7-8 hours of sleep. Less than seven hours do not allow the body to repair itself. More than nine hours may signal lack of challenge in your life.

Eat a Balanced Diet: Eat breakfast like a king, lunch like a prince and a supper like a pauper.

Get a Physical Examination: Get a complete physical from your doctor. Let him/her know your plan and ask your doctor if you are in a physical condition to take on the intended exercise.

Select the Exercise You Like: Some people like walking, hiking, jogging, riding a bike, dancing, swimming or playing tennis. Tennis may not be your racket. Choose the exercise you enjoy doing for at least 30 minutes. Your heart rate must rise to 75% of your maximum capacity in order to strengthen your heart muscles. Walking happens to be the best and the safest exercise. Moreover, it does not require a committee meeting to get started. You should be able to walk at least two miles a day in about 30 minutes. Exercise at least six days a week. Some suggest three days. Getting three days of exercise is like living on a minimum wage. Can you afford it?

Be Patient: Remember, it took you a long time to be in your present condition. It will take some time for you to get back to health. Never be in a hurry or fall for unbelievably high-risk, quick scams and shortcut programs that would have you look like Barbie doll or adorable "Ken" in a matter of days or weeks. Take your time. If you loose weight in a hurry, it is bound to return and stay with you. Many people have lost thousands of pounds and they are still overweight. Start slow and build up. Morning is generally the best time but do it whenever possible, as long as the temperature is below 85 degrees. It pays to have a buddy to exercise with but don't wait to build an exercise fan club before getting started. You will make many friends on the road or in a gym. Get started and be consistent.

SOMETHING TO THINK ABOUT

Exercise is the single most important thing you can do for yourself to prevent disease, and live longer now.

Build Your Own "Mountain of Joy" and Climb It Daily

MANY PEOPLE ARE suffocating in a cesspool of negativity. They wake up expecting hell to break loose any time. They ride on a horse named "Lame Blame" that keeps them going in circles. If they win 95% of the time, they are miserable thinking of the 5% of the time they did not win. If their stock broker calls to give them the news that their stock made 10% this month, they panic, anticipating that it is not going to do well in the coming month. If their doctor gives them a clean bill of health, they immediately add, "Who knows what will happen on my way home?" If such a person is selected vice president of an organization, he wonders why he was not selected as the president. There is no good news for such a sewer-swimming person. If you work for or with such people, you cannot win regardless of the outcome. They are miserable and they will take you down with them. You need to learn to build your own mountain of joy. Here are a few tips.

To build your *"Mountain of Joy,"* repeat the exercise described earlier. Take thirty minutes before you go to bed at night and thirty minutes in the morning before starting your day. Find a comfortable place in your home. Sit on the floor with your eyes closed and your hands in your lap. Go as far back as you can remember and think of all the best things that have happened in your life. The helpful people you have met, the wonderful places you have visited, the inspiring sites you have seen, great friends you have made, little joys you experienced when you helped someone along the way, the sunset, the sunrise you have admired and the times when you put a smile on someone's face. Think of the wonderful challenges you faced and met successfully. Recall the opportunities you had in your career to make friends and help people. Think of the time you lightened the burden of someone who was carrying a heavy load. Think of the occasion when you shared your sandwich with a hungry homeless person or a colleague who did not have the money to buy lunch. What about the time you paid an extra dollar at the grocery store to help a person who wanted the milk for her baby but did not have enough money? And how about the time you were standing in line at a movie theatre and the family ran short of one ticket for their children? Don't forget the time you made a "Care Pack" for soldiers fighting overseas. Do you remember the time you gave blood at the local blood bank to save a teenager who had a car crash in your neighborhood? Did you not have a great day when you marched in the "Heart Saver's" parade to raise funds for your local Heart Association? Finally, did you not see that special glow on your face when you joined the neighbors to help rebuild the women's shelter in your community with the help of the organization "Habitat for Humanity?"

As you recall all these wonderful experiences, you will discover your "Mountain of Joy" that you have either forgotten or taken for granted. Climb your mountain daily and get high on life. The journey of life is full of thorns and flowers. Just ignore the thorns and admire the flowers. Our negative thoughts are usually prompted by our encounter with people who invoke negative memories or by recalling unpleasant experiences of the past. Play only the positive tapes.

SOMETHING TO THINK ABOUT

We all have a choice to stare at a pool of problems or a "Mountain of Joy." What is your choice?

Floss Your Joy Daily

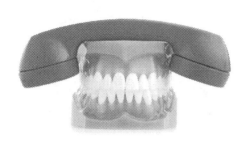

HAVE YOU BEEN to your dentist lately? When was the last time you had your teeth cleaned? I saw a great sign in a Dentist's office, "If you are not true to your teeth, they will be false to you." Another sign read, "You don't have to floss all your teeth, only the ones you want to keep." This dentist takes time to teach his patients the secrets of maintaining good dental health. I recall his counseling one of his patients about plaque build-up, receding gums, and how these problems were distorting his bite and facial expressions. He reminded the patient that he needed to floss his teeth daily after each meal in order to prevent plaque build-up. When plaque surrounds the tooth, it pulls calcium out and allows bacteria to penetrate the tooth, thus, leaving the tooth unprotected. Furthermore, it erodes enamel that guards the tooth and keeps it strong. Plaque damages the outer coating of the tooth and harms its structure. It prevents nutrients from getting to the tooth and eventually a person develops a toothache. By removing plaque, a person can improve his dental health and delay a host of dental problems. My dentist advised me to floss my teeth every time I eat.

I have been thinking about the lessons I can learn from the flossing process. Undesirable thoughts or people around us are quite similar to plaque build-up. They begin to brainwash us and distort our potential. Unless we remain vigilant, we find ourselves unprotected and eventually, give in. It would pay to make a list of people, places, things and events that compromise our joy and develop a better relationship with them. It is important to identify times and events that make us unhappy, and develop constructive ways to deal with them. Don't allow any plaque to build around your joy. The longer it lingers, the greater the chance of its developing cavities in your joy, eventually rotting your joy totally. Scrape off the plaque as soon as you discover it. Brush up on your joy daily. The best way to keep your joy shining is to adopt an attitude of gratitude, a spirit of forgiveness and an intense hunger to benefit others. Keep a happy disposition. If you keep smiling, people will wonder what's up your sleeves!

Removing plaque build-up requires vigilance. It is inconvenient to floss. It takes time and effort. We get busy and, frankly, lazy! It is humiliating to look in the mirror and see how much excess baggage we may be carrying. Just as it is not comfortable to go to the dentist, it is not easy to see our short-comings and part with them. It is equally difficult to eliminate the company of people who compromise your joy. We are afraid to lose their friendship and support. However, plaque is not a friend of the tooth. The role of plaque is to weaken the tooth and give its owner a tooth- ache. To have undesirable thoughts and people around us is to have a bumper crop of headaches that erode our joy. It is an art to safeguard our time, resources and energy from negative and unproductive forces. However, in pursuit of excellence one must remain on guard to ensure that the journey of life is not compromised or detoured. Floss your joy daily.

SOMETHING TO THINK ABOUT

Do you have the courage to floss away the human plaque that surrounds your life? Think about it!

Water Your Joy Daily and See It Grow

I WAS VERY fortunate to grow up at a farm. My parents grew vegetables. When I was about eight years of age, my father gave me a small plot of land and told me that I could plant whatever I wanted as long as I took care of it. I planted peanuts, potatoes and watermelons. I spent much of my time after school at my vegetable patch. I was not fully aware about the time it took for the seeds to germinate, and my patience was wearing real thin just waiting. Finally the plants appeared. However, I was very anxious to see the fruit of my labor. I could see the flowers and then tiny watermelons on the watermelon vine, but I was not happy about my peanut and potato crop. A few times, I dug under the peanut and potato plants to see if there was any growth.

During the hot summer days, occasionally, I would forget to water my vegetable patch and the plants would wilt. My father sat me down one day and reviewed the principles of successful farming. He advised me that **(a)** I needed to be responsible to look after my own vegetable patch. **(b)** I must be patient and quit disturbing the roots by digging under the plants. **(c)** I must pull out weeds so they would not steal the food from the plants and grow stronger and choke the plants. **(d)** I must not neglect the plants even for a day. During the summer time, I should water my plants daily either early in the morning or in the evening. Watering the plants was one of the most important steps, father advised me.

I have often thought of that vegetable patch. I can picture my father teaching me simple lessons to grow my peanut, potato and watermelon crop. So it is with growing our happiness. When we first fall in love with someone, it's just like planting a tiny seed that may someday grow and give us a full crop of joyful experiences. Just like my vegetable patch, it requires personal responsibility to tend to small details that make a big difference in building joyful relationships. We cannot force our love or friendship on others. We can plant seeds and nurture them and with patience, see them grow. We cannot hurry people to fall in love with us, run to embrace us, or become our business partners. We also cannot dig into their personal lives; that would be like digging the roots to see the growth. Give people the freedom to share with us, only if they wish. We must carefully evaluate our interactions with others and weed out our habits that may irritate others and strain our relationship.

You are welcome to do your own research, but according to my observation, the people we tend to neglect the most are the ones who live with us, work with us or the ones we consider our close friends. Seek opportunities to thank them and you will harvest a bumper crop of joy. We tend to be liberal in acknowledging our shortcoming when we hurt a stranger; however, we seem to demand greater understanding from those we live with and those whom we hurt the most. The people we live with also have feelings that are easily hurt. In fact, we need to be more vigilant in recognizing, acknowledging and making amends when we hurt them.

SOMETHING TO THINK ABOUT

Each time you introduce joy to a sad soul, you also water the thirsty and dry corners of your own heart and make it a fertile soil for joy to multiply a thousand times.

Light Up Your Joy Daily

ANDY WORKED AT Family Motors in Bakersfield, California. He managed the auto-reconditioning department. He had a perpetual smile on his face, regardless of the circumstances. I used to edit the Company newsletter. In order to bolster employee morale, I offered a $25 award to anyone who might catch Andy grouchy and without a smile. Just the fact that I showed so much confidence in him, it served as a mega dose of adrenalin for Andy. He would walk the campus with such a positive attitude that people named him "Mr. Sunshine." A few colleagues jokingly asked if I had placed Andy on some special "Happiness Pill" to keep him so excited about life. Everyone enjoyed working with him. He was always on time and eager to lend a hand to anyone in need. I had the privilege to invite Andy and his family over for dinner a few times. His son Josh, age four, had already been programmed to be like his father. Josh would volunteer to distribute books or set silverware for the table. If we were not able to assign any chores to little Josh, he would be pacing up and down asking what more could he do. Observing his father, little Josh had learned to be cheerful and helpful. It was a delight to have the young Josh at our group discussions. Josh's energy and electrifying positive personality made many adults have a second thought when they were tempted to gripe about their circumstances.

Happy people are like the candle or a light bulb. They light up the place no matter where they go and regardless of their environment. Just as the candle does not fight with darkness, they don't have to announce their presence. By their very presence, they signal a different aura. They add flavor and enhance the value of everyone and everything they touch. They are a blessing to people within their friendship circle. People enjoy their company. If you had a choice, would you choose to be with people who specialize in criticizing and bringing people down or would you rather be with those who give you a lift? I bet you would choose the second option. So would I.

By lighting up the life of people around us, we would light up our own life. Why not start with your family who put up with you in spite of all your shortcomings? Don't forget your gardener, mailman, your child's teacher, and your boss. By lightening the burden of those around us, our own journey of life would become easier. By shedding rays of sunshine on the lives of people who sit and sulk in darkness and gloom, you would light a candle within your own soul and its internal warmth would make your face glow for everyone to see. Remember, a candle does not have to argue or prove its virtue, it just glows! Studies after studies have proven that happy people get sick less often and recover much faster. The body rejuvenates at a much faster pace when we are positive and joyful in comparison to when we are grouchy and critical.

Would you like to be a candle or a wet blanket?

SOMETHING TO THINK ABOUT

What steps do you plan to take in order to become a candle to light up your home or place of work or your neighborhood?

How would you demonstrate your confidence in people around you so they may become a beacon of light instead of a winter cloud?

Fertilize Your Joy Daily

GROWING UP AT a farm taught me many valuable lessons to help me along life's journey. My father used to plant a certain type of fast growing grass and when it would grow about two feet tall, he would plough it right back into the soil. I used to ask him for his reason to waste all those seeds. He would reply, "My son, we need to feed the soil in order for it to grow a healthier crop." He would also purchase various types of fertilizers to enrich the soil. Seeing my father work so hard to prepare the soil for planting the intended crop was always discouraging to me. I wanted my dad to plant vegetables, corn or wheat quickly so I could see it grow. I used to wonder why dad took so much time in preparing the soil. When dad would finally plant the crop, it grew so abundantly that other farmers used to visit my dad and ask for his secret of growing such a healthy crop. I often heard my dad say to them, "Spending time to prepare the soil is like buying an insurance policy to have a bumper crop at harvest time." My dad was absolutely right! Once we planted a cauliflower crop. Some of the heads were nearly eighteen inches in diameter.

This little brush with farming at an early age taught me that if I want my joy to grow, my relationship with people must be genuine and have deep roots. I cannot have superficial interactions with people around me and expect a bumper crop of happiness. According to the University of Chicago's National Opinion Research Center, people with five or more close friends were 50% more likely to describe themselves as "Very happy" than respondents with fewer friends. People who have a loving marriage, 40% of those described themselves to be "Very happy" in comparison to only 26% of those who were unmarried. Connection with a community group or a religious congregation also was a factor in predicting the level of one's happiness. Happiness grows as we invest ourselves in enriching the live of others.

The same study also surveyed 800 college alumni and learned that classmates who valued high income, job success, and prestige more than close friends and love, were twice as likely to be "Fairly" or "Very" unhappy. Many people try to buy friendships and relationships. They throw money, at people to earn their loyalty and closeness. Sonja Lyubomirsky, a researcher at the University of California at Riverside, told a Chicago Tribune reporter, "It's definitely not money," that predicts one's happiness. "It's not he who dies with the most toys that wins. It's he who has the most time to play with his toys, and the most fun playing with them, who wins." Throwing money at people to buy their warmth and friendship is like dumping horse manure on your flower plants and burning them. Growing your joy requires the investment of time, unconditional love, patience, forgiveness and the ability to start over. These are to a relationship what fertilizer would be to the soil that produces bumper crops.

(**Source:** Dayana Yochim's article, "Money=Happiness," quoted in The Motley Fool.Com, September 18, 2004).

SOMETHING TO THINK ABOUT

Are you investing enough time on activities that would grow your joy in life?

Take an inventory of the things that may be depriving you of joyful relationships.

Plant Your Joy throughout the Day

O VER THE YEARS, among my many assignments, I have had the oversight of community relations and customer care. I am sure you have heard that the "customer is always right." While I believe that a customer is always right from his/her perspective, many customers have a tough time expressing their frustrations constructively. Every now and then I meet people who seem to have been awakened by a bad dream. In a three-year long study of white collar government workers, I discovered that 40% of them had severe personal and family problems, such as drug abuse, excessive alcohol use, child abuse, domestic violence, child-custody battles, or trouble with the law. Some were dodging the bill collectors, having problems with the Internal Revenue Services or facing personal health problems. Four in ten persons were unhappy for one reason or the other. Most of them kept their problems in their front pocket or in the top drawer in the office.

At one of the blue-collar industries where I worked, more than 50% of the workers were either divorced or in the process of getting unhitched. In short, the work place was infested with broken hearts, aborted dreams, people burdened with truckloads of disappointments, suffering from broken promises, stagnant marriages and running around with short fuses. Is there a need of some joy in a jaundiced world around you? Of course! Our world needs joy more than the Sahara Desert needs the rain. In order to brighten our own lives, we need to plant the seeds of joy in lives around us that have hardened like barren soil due to decades of drought.

Consider every heart you encounter a fertile soil for you to plant seeds of joy. The more seeds you plant in the hearts around you, the more joyful grins you will witness around you. Plant generously. Don't count the seeds, just scatter them randomly and see them grow! Search for people who may be allergic to joy and creatively introduce joy to them. Send them flowers; surprise them with a home-baked cake, a loaf of bread, a thank you note, a get-well card, and a ride to the store or just a visit to admire them as your neighbors. Remember, no one needs joy more than those who have never met her. Plant your joy every where you go.

A wise man once said, "He who waits for fair weather to plant, will not reap." He also advised, "Plant in the morning and also at night. Who knows which one will germinate?" It means that we should plant our joy even if we have to go against the wind. When you return good for evil, you are planting seeds of joy. You are planting the seeds of joy when you wish your enemy only the best of life, help someone in need, go easy on someone who may be at fault, stay cool when you have every right to blow your top, and send a nice encouraging note to someone who is down-hearted. To plant your joy, give people a good deal and a good deal more, think noble thoughts about someone who hates your shadow, be kind to the poor, be protective of the weak, be patient with the rich, be peaceful when you have all the reasons to scream your lungs out with anger, and wear a smile when you feel like crying. You will not always find a fertile soil to plant your joy, plant it anyway. People may not reciprocate your smile, but smile at them anyway.

SOMETHING TO THINK ABOUT

Think about the things you did at work today to multiply your joy and repeat them often.

Don't Let the
Weeds Choke
Your Joy

MISERY LOVES COMPANY. Miserable people usually go around robbing others of joyful experiences. Don't share your moping with others. Twenty percent don't care and 80% are happy that you are miserable, just like them. Weed out any negative thoughts or ideas that would not benefit you or others around you. Remember, if you don't weed your flower garden, the weeds will choke the flowers. Be heartless and uproot the undesirable plants before they overtake and choke your flower garden. Learn to identify seeds of such plants early and don't allow anyone to plant them in your garden. Remember the old saying, "As a person thinks in his mind, so is he." Keep the mind clean and fresh. The enemy will try to plant discontentment, a spirit of criticism, disharmony and discord. Watch out! Big people think about ideas, average people think about things and little people think about other people. Be a big person! When you see people devouring people, steer clear. Don't join the gossip gang. Critical people are like cancer cells and termites. They destroy families and organizations. I call them "Dream Robbers." Watch out for negative and critical people. They are like weeds. Here are a few suggestions as to how you may keep the weeds away from your garden of joy.

Don't share anything negative about people who are absent.

If the glove doesn't fit, don't wear it – you may make holes in it.

Don't try to push your solutions to solve other people's problems.

Start the day with a plan and end it with an assessment to improve it.

Don't get puffed up and fall for empty words when people praise you.

Never peddle an idea unless you are certain it will stand the test of truth.

Stop rumor mongers who don't have the evidence to back up their claims.

Never lose your cool when your child fights with your neighbor's children.

Guard your time carefully – don't hang around with negative news makers.

Don't discuss your problem, except with the one who can help you solve it.

Offer to link the back-biters immediately to the person they are disparaging.

If you want people to change for the better, show them how; don't tell them.

Don't stay silent when someone is receiving undue criticism in your presence.

Never give people an insincere compliment and distort their picture of reality.

Don't ever down a person because he doesn't agree with your line of thinking.

When others share their problems with you, ask questions and help them think.

Congratulate your competitor when he/she outsmarts you and wins the contest.

Think before you speak, better yet, consider the time and place before speaking.

Don't believe anything you hear unless you can back it up with your observation.

Don't listen to negative things about people who are not there to defend themselves.

Don't respond with emotions – get your mind in
gear before your tongue goes to work.

SOMETHING TO THINK ABOUT

Think about the principles cited above and see your garden of joy bloom.

Don't neglect to weed out what threatens your joy – the price is exorbitant.

Root Your Joy Deeper Every Day

JOY IS NOT an artificial and temporary grin. It is the result of being at peace with the people we live with, work with and, most of all, being at peace with the person who stares at us in the mirror. When joy is rooted in our heart, it does not easily fade away because of other people's mood swings. Such joy holds its ground even if other people change their minds about us. It is not easily disturbed when we face rejection, neglect, criticism, or abandonment. True joy that is rooted in self-confidence is not contingent upon a cheerleader to reassure us.

So let your joy grow deeper roots every day that it may withstand hormonal changes. Here are a few suggestions to help your joy grow deeper roots.

Choose Joy As Your Natural Companion. Joy has a peculiar habit. It never hugs those who don't choose to embrace it. Choose to be a happy person, and if you are happy, let your face know it. When joy becomes your natural friend, it is deeper and not easily shaken because of life's day-to-day challenges.

Anchor Your Joy to Things of Real Value. If we base our joy in having money, then what will happen to our joy when the money is gone? If we tie it to having a prestigious job, what would happen if we lose that job? If we depend on others to make us happy, what if they don't show up? If our joy depends on the praise others bestow on us, then what will happen when others ignore us? Our joy must be rooted in a genuine purpose for living. It is enhanced by an opportunity to make the best use of our talents and skills to serve others. By serving others we experience a true sense of accomplishment.

One of the ways I have found very useful in growing deeper roots for my joy has been visiting sick people in hospitals and convalescent facilities. I remember once when I was in Maryland. I went to a nursing home. The moment I walked into the room I saw two ladies seated on their beds. As soon as they saw me, their faces lighted up and one of them remarked to the other, "See, I told you he would come. We are going to go to dinner. He is going to give me a special treat today." I had never met them before but just to see them happy made my happiness meter climb.

Share Your Joy With Joy-Challenged People. One of the fastest and best ways to grow deeper roots for your joy is to seek opportunities to share joyful experiences with those who even seem to be miserable if they are not miserable. Use your creativity to provide opportunities for people who have a hard time to crack a smile or say something positive. Your joy will grow deeper and your life will take on a special meaning when you help unhappy people experience joy. As you dispel darkness, your own world will light up like the crack of dawn. ***Happiness is growing wild all around us; I have always wondered why so many people live in such misery. Happiness is dancing around us looking for a partner. I wonder why so many stand on the sideline, lonely and sad!***

SOMETHING TO THINK ABOUT

Find joy in things that uplift others around you and see your own joy grow deeper!

Invite Joy to Kitchen Conversations

KITCHEN CONVERSATION: INVITE JOY to all your meals. Unhappiness around the table at meal times leads to a host of stomach disorders. A stressful environment seriously affects the flow of gastric juices needed for digestion. If the meal goes to the stomach and the gastric juice does not show up, the food will not digest. If the gastric juice shows up and there is no food, it will drill holes in the stomach linings, resulting in peptic ulcers. America leads the world in stomach-related diseases. Meal times should not be used to scold the children or get even with your spouse. It is not the time to settle big family feuds.

Kitchen Chores: The family needs to work together so that no member of the house is over working or fatigued by entertaining the rest. Some women, out of the goodness of their hearts, would like to do it all by themselves. Use your leadership skills and teach the rest of the family to help in the kitchen. Determine what they can do just as well as you can and delegate those tasks to them. When you try to do it all, there is a tendency to get physically exhausted and irritable. This creates bad air around the table at meal times. It's not healthy.

Create an Air of Joy and Surprise: Use your creativity to set the table with a touch of class – making it as attractive as possible. Use meal times as an opportunity to surprise one another, to show love. You can place some love notes under each plate, place some flower petals around the plate or hide a question under each place mat and ask for a response. There are many ways to make meal time an event that will give you a boost.

Have an Attitude of Gratitude: An attitude of gratitude must pervade the air. There are many who have to search for their bread daily. If they did not earn something each day, they cannot buy food for their family. There are millions who go to bed hungry. We live in a free country where the system is designed in such a way that NO ONE WHO IS TRULY NEEDY ever has to go to bed hungry. And, don't take your gifts for granted. Someone had to work to pay for the nice meal you are eating. Someone had to prepare it. Why not thank those who bless you?

Share Joy as a Regular Dish at All Meals: When sitting around the breakfast, lunch or dinner table, take the opportunity to serve an extra helping of JOY to all around you. Even if you are eating with your friends at the office, use those moments to brighten your colleague's life. Use meal times to recall the good in people around you and commend them for it. Thank your spouse, your children, their friends and anyone eating with you. Don't be selfish. Meals eaten without JOY contribute to a host of physical and interpersonal problems. Don't drive JOY away by having critical kitchen conversations. Meal time should not be allowed to become a family feud game. It is a time to reaffirm one another, catch up on family news, brain storm about weekend activities and show love for one another.

SOMETHING TO THINK ABOUT

Make a resolution to help in the kitchen and offer assistance without invitation. If you do most of the cooking, train other members and delegate tasks and show appreciation.

Send Joy on a Journey with Everyone

MY WIFE USUALLY makes lunches for my children when they go to school or snowboarding. However, whenever I get an opportunity to make a lunch for my wife or children, I try to slip in short love notes in their lunch bags. I remember writing one such note for my daughter when she was in high school. It just said, "I love you. I will be praying for you, love, Dad!" For many years that note remained stuck on the wall near her bed. We can never comprehend the value of little notes and the JOY these add to the lives of the people around us. During a job transition, I was home for a few days. I began to fix lunches for my son and daughter. I would faithfully put a love note in my daughter's lunch bag but not in my son's. I thought that he was too old for such notes and may not care to read them. One day after school, my daughter remarked, "Myron is wondering how come he does not get any love notes from dad." I quickly learned that age never dims our hunger for love. At all stages of our journey, we need people around us to reassure us that they love and care for us, that life is worth living in spite of all its challenges, and that it is worth waking up in the morning. It is the love of people around us that keeps us going when the cold, chilly and rainy weather makes our path slippery.

Years ago I heard a story of a father who attended a seminar. The speaker gave each attendee two ribbons with the following words: "I love you. You are #1." He asked that they give one of the ribbons to someone they did not get along with. Upon arriving home, the father saw that the light was still on in his son's room. He knocked and heard the voice, "What do you want?" The father politely replied that he wanted to give him something. The boy cracked the door opened slightly and took the ribbon. Next morning, when the father was about to leave for work, the boy ran to him with tears and thanked him for the ribbon. Then he related to the father that last night he was preparing to kill himself because he did not think anyone loved him anymore. The ribbon saved his life. Don't ever underestimate the power of expressing your love to your family or to the people you meet on the journey of your life.

Send JOY on a journey with everyone you meet. Make memories worth recalling in case you never meet them again. I often think of the thousands who died in America on 9/11, 2001. Many must have left their homes with unfinished business. Stay current in all your accounts of life. Each night, sleep with your account in balance. Audit your account before you leave the house, the office or the marketplace. Ask yourself, "Am I leaving behind a gift that would add a bit of joy to the people. What emotions would they express when they think of my encounter with them? Will they make someone's day happier because of the joyful experience I provided them? Would they welcome someone with open arms because I made them feel better about themselves?" Your encounter with people can leave them either ***bitter or better***. If they feel better than when they came to see you, they will spread a ray of hope to those they encounter.

SOMETHING TO THINK ABOUT

If life is worth living, it's worth living with JOY. Take JOY with you everywhere you go.

Wherever you are, think of ways to multiply your JOY by sharing it with others.

Take JOY to Work Every Day

IN CALIFORNIA THERE are days designated as "Take your child to work with you. Take your dog to work with you." I wish we had a National Day – "Take JOY to work with you." The American Cancer Society celebrates the "Great American Smoke-out" day each year, with the hope that if Americans can quit smoking for a day, they may like it and quit it for life. It is my hope that everyone would take JOY to work one day and get hooked on it, and never again part with its company. I hope that JOY would stick with you like the two layers of your skin.

According to a recent workplace poll, over 50% of the people don't like their jobs. Numbers were even higher in some parts of the country. Imagine a person not liking his/her job! Would they rather be without a job? I have not seen many who are jumping for joy because they don't have a job. You may not find the job you like, but you can always love the job you have. People who don't like their job, for them JOB = JUST OVER BROKE. Their spirit is already broken, leaving them incapable to add value to anyone or anything they touch. They spend at least nine hours at the office stewing in unhappiness and arriving home like a burnt toast to drive JOY out of the lives of their family members. You need JOY on the JOB. Don't leave home without her.

Add JOY To The Life Of Your Boss: Owners and managers have the responsibility for the company and its employees, but they have no control over how things actually work. They have to always depend on others to make their vision a reality. If things go well, the employees want all the credit. If things go bad, they pin it on their supervisors and owners. Being an owner or a manager is a no-win-job. Your boss and your immediate supervisor could stand a lift. Share JOY with them. Don't seek them out only when you have a problem.

Add JOY To The Life Of Your Co-workers: If you could read the minds of your co-workers, you may need a ton of pain killers. Over 40% of your co-workers in a white collar industry are battling severe family or personal problems. Many people around you are simply "Walking Dead." If you could deliver a paycheck to their homes without their having to show up for work, they would be grateful. For many, work may be the only thing going for them. It may be the JOY they experience at work that keeps them going at home.

When I was working with a large health service agency in California, I had an employee whom I considered to be a "Model" for everyone to follow. One day, while I was away for a conference in Sacramento, California, I got a call that she had committed suicide. I quickly packed my bags and returned to my office to see what had happened. There was a note in my desk drawer from the young lady. It read, "Dear Dr. Massey, I want to thank you for all the support you have given me in making my work a pleasant place. However, the rest of my life has gotten so bad that I cannot continue. Sorry I had to put you and the staff through this." Take JOY to work with you every day – someone is waiting and crying for it! Behind those smiles and grins, many are nursing a wounded and a broken heart. They need a lift.

SOMETHING TO THINK ABOUT

Think about ways you can add JOY to the people around you at work. Be liberal in sharing your JOY. Sharing it with others is the best way to multiply your own JOY!

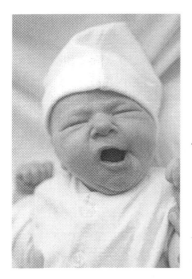

Sleep With JOY Every Night

WHEN I WAS a child my father used to say, "Don't let the sun go down on your anger. Fix the problem before you go to bed or you will have bad dreams." At the end of the day, take an inventory of what has transpired throughout the day. Evaluate the decisions you made and see how you could improve if you had to make the same choices again. Review your encounters with people and assess if your transactions had the outcomes you expected. Take a mind-walk and see the results of your day's work and determine if you did your best or not. In case you short-changed someone during the day, call the person and make amends. By evaluating your day and taking corrective actions prior to closing your books, you will have cleared your deck. It will help you become a better person to do greater things the next day. You will have a good sleep. You will wake up rested and renewed to tackle new challenges and take advantage of new opportunities.

As you review your day's account, you are likely to recall instances where you did not achieve the desired results. It is conceivable that it was the other party that deserved the credit for the compromised outcome. The tendency is to wait for those who were at fault to come forward and make things right. If we are not at fault, we tend to stand our ground and expect the offending party to take the first step. This logic seems to pass the legal test. However, if you want to "BUILD A BETTER YOU," then you may have to dispense with legalities and go beyond the average mentality. You don't have to agree with a viewpoint that is not right, but you can still remain agreeable and respect the other person's way of looking at things from their vantage point. You can take the first step to clear the air.

Going through this soul searching exercise at the end of the day is critical in order to build a strong foundation for better outcomes the next day. Failure to evaluate our day leads us to relive all those bad experiences subconsciously at night while we think we are asleep. It robs us of the energy and enthusiasm that would be required of us to face the new day. Nothing is better than going to bed at night with JOY. (If there is a reader whose name is Joy, please understand that I am using the word "JOY" in this chapter as a synonym for happiness and not as a personal pronoun).

If you sleep with JOY at night, you are likely to wake up in her arms in the morning to start the day with enthusiasm and excitement. Many go to bed thinking about their bills, unsettled quarrels, unhappy experiences, and a wide variety of unfinished business. Instead of being negative, be creative, and by your example, show a better way. Crown the day with a happy note. Going to bed without JOY can deprive you of pleasant dreams and give you a bumper crop of nightmares. You may wake up tired and lifeless. Going to bed unhappy can contribute to high blood pressure and a host of associated maladies. It will affect your digestive process. Clear your mind so JOY may dwell in it.

SOMETHING TO THINK ABOUT

A good night's sleep prevents a host of illnesses and prolongs life. Don't compromise it!

The Boy Who Wanted Corn

H E WAS BORN in a small village in Mexico to a family where his mother was the main bread-winner to care for eleven children. As he recalls it, when he was six, his mother sent him on a mission over the hill to borrow corn from a neighbor so that she could fix a meal for the family. On the way, he sat on a rock to rest a while and looked into the sky asking the most probing question ever posed to the Great Spirit by philosophers and pundits – "Why do others have corn and we don't?" He was not only a curious researcher but a sharp businessman. He struck a bargain with the Great Spirit. "If you give me corn, I will share it with those who need it." How many six-year-olds do you know who ask for a blessing so they could share it unselfishly to meet the needs of the less fortunate among us?

The Great Spirit landed him and his entire family in America six years after he bargained for corn. His first job to sow corn was washing cars at a dealership. He arrived on his bicycle earlier than anyone else, made sure that the place was ready for the Company guests, and worked on each car as though he was going to personally ride in it to his wedding ceremony. The owner watched him carefully and predicted that someday he would own a dealership and have plenty of corn. In 1993, at the age of 32 he acquired his first used-car dealership, not knowing that by 2003, he would own an empire of nine dealerships, a restaurant, golf course, real estate company and a host of other business ventures. He asked for corn but the Great Spirit blessed him with a corn-field. His life reminded me of the ancient story when a boy named Solomon was crowned king and was asked by God what he wanted. He asked for wisdom to serve his people rightly. God told him that because of his unselfish request, he would grant him wisdom and also wealth beyond his expectation.

The boy who wanted corn to share it with others has kept the promise he made with the Great Spirit. His life is more than money. His secret of growth is imbedded in his service to his community. Service is the bridge we build for others to walk over to us so we may have the privilege to serve them and be blessed in return. Each year, Jose awards scholarships to students, partners with a host of churches, civic clubs and community organizations to improve the lives of the less fortunate. "We are not in the business of selling cars, instead, we are in the business of making friends and helping people," says Jose Arredondo. When I first began to associate with Jose, he gave me the responsibility to distribute his "Corn" to the needy. "Never turn down any request for help," he advised me. "When we submit a customer's application to a bank, I don't like to hear that the customer does not qualify, instead, I like to hear that he does not qualify for a $20,000 vehicle but he can qualify for $15,000 or $10,000. Don't ever close the door of hope on people." It is this philosophy that distinguishes Jose from others.

If everyone had "abundant thinking," this world would have more blessed people. People with abundant thinking put others first, let others win, let others have the last word, and become people builder.

SOMETHING TO THINK ABOUT

It is by putting others first that we distinguish ourselves from the herd.

Invest in the "Soil of Your Soul" (Part I)

YOUR COMMUNITY IS the "soil of your soul." It gave you birth and depends on you for its nurture, service and survival. Be active in preserving mother earth and its inhabitants. Here are a few noble examples of how you may enrich the soil of your soul, give back to your community and achieve true greatness.

Actress Angelina Jolie: November, 2004 issue of Reader's Digest featured a story, "Angelina Jolie's Double Life." The Hollywood's superstar that appeared in "Lara Croft, Tomb Raider," "Girl Interrupted," and plays the mother of Alexander in the film "Alexander," lives an amazingly exciting life outside of her movie world. She is a U.N. Ambassador to Cambodia to visit refugee camps. It is inspiring to see her in action, seated on the floor, surrounded by hundreds of poor children, and administering the most vital survival tonic – love. She seems to be the happiest when she can put a smile on the face of a lonely child. Her commitment to give back to the community is punctuated by the fact that she adopted one of the orphan boys. Angelina feels most satisfied when a child feels safe, secure and loved. Leaving behind the five-star hotel luxury of America and going to poverty-stricken refugee camps in Cambodia and identifying with the victims of human pain and suffering reveals the true strength of her character. Angelina is giving back to the community and feeling more blessed than by playing make-believe roles on movie sets and winning Academy Awards.

Former President Jimmy Carter: I have been greatly impressed by the example of former President Jimmy Carter – another great American hero. After leaving his office, he has devoted his life to being a goodwill ambassador to the world. He has visited many poverty-stricken countries and helped organize efforts to improve lives of people around the globe. He has worked behind the scenes to promote public policies in various countries to alleviate human suffering. He has fought against racism, separatism, prejudice and selfishness. His efforts with the "Habitat for Humanity" have provided shelter for thousands who would otherwise be victims to cold and harsh environmental conditions. Many retired government workers peddle the globe promoting themselves and their book deals, while the former President has championed the cause of human equality and advocated a better quality of life for all. Watching him work shoulder-to-shoulder with natives makes you proud to be a citizen of the world.

Buffalo Banks in India is another example of an innovative way to give back to the community. Under the direction of Dr. Edwin Dass, President of Roorkee Adventist College, in India, "Students and health professionals from Central and Southern California have adopted two villages and established a "Buffalo Bank" for widows. The recipients of buffalos are carefully educated about how to care for the animal. The family is able to sell the milk and make a living. When the buffalo yields a calf, the family cares for it until it is old enough to be gifted to another family to help start another family business. This project has resulted in a double blessing: (a) The host college is providing students a "Service Learning" experience and introducing them to the joys of investing back into the community. (b) The business community is partnering with local village folks to demonstrate the true purpose of education – building better communities. The group has also established an adult-literacy and occupational center for needy children.

SOMETHING TO THINK ABOUT

Is this world a better place to live because of the investment you are making to improve it?

Invest in the "Soil of Your Soul" (Part II)

EVERY NOW AND then I meet people who have given up on the world. They believe that the world is inhabited primarily by selfish and self-serving inconsiderate people who live by the principle – "Mine is mine and yours is yours, until I get it." They see no light at the end of the tunnel. In reality, this planet is full of individuals who are gifted with hearts as wide as the Atlantic Ocean that flow with generosity. Just listening to their life-stories inspires me to think better, be a better person and live with hope for a brighter future. Let me share with you an inspiring example.

Debi Faris-Cifelli and her husband Steve of Calimesa, California, operate a cemetery for abused, neglected and abandoned infants. In 2001, a California law made it possible for young mothers to leave their unwanted babies at Fire Departments and other selected places without fear of being prosecuted. Over 107 babies have been abandoned since the law was first enacted. Some babies have survived and some have died. Debi and Steve have only 95 plots at their cemetery. They have sobbed and suffered heartache while burying 70 of these abandoned and diseased infants in their cemetery. Their passion to serve distressed young girls, whose parents obviously were not able to provide them the needed support, has compelled them to hold car washes, bake sales and write grants for assistance. They have struggled to support their mission of compassion.

On December 8, 2004, Debi and her husband received a call that made them dance with joy. The caller announced that she had won the lottery jackpot for $27 million. "Maybe it's the children saying 'Thank you' for taking care of them when nobody else would," Debi said. "It's a gift and one for which we feel an awesome responsibility," she added. I listened to the radio interview and heard Debi say to her husband, "Honey, we have always been rich. We were being prepared for this time to receive the gift." Before you read further, close your eyes, take a moment and think how you would spend the money if you were to win $27 million. What do you think Debi and Steve decided to do with the money?

Debi and her husband were full of ideas about how to spend the lottery money on anyone but themselves. They decided to establish two perpetual scholarships in the name of each of the seventy children buried in their cemetery. They wanted the funds to help educate the troubled teens to cope with their challenges. They also decided to use part of the money to possibly build a shelter for pregnant teens. If the seventy little kids could see Debi and her husband, they would see them dancing with excitement that they would now have the resources to support their mission to teens and abandoned children (Source: The Bakersfield Californian, December 9, 2004).

Debi serves the Inland Empire, a three-county region in Southern California (Los Angeles, Riverside and San Bernardino). In spite of the fact that Debi and her husband will receive only $9 million lump sum of the $27 million jackpot after taxes, their first love is to support their crusade to help abused and abandoned children. Giving back to the community comes naturally to Debi and Steve. This is what I mean by investing in nurturing the soil of our soul.

SOMETHING TO THINK ABOUT

Nothing detours people of character from their life-passion. When they receive material blessings, they simply find it easier to pursue their purpose for life. What is your passion?

Invest in the "Soil of Your Soul" (Part III)

THERE IS AN ancient story of a boy who was hated by his brothers. The brothers first wanted to kill him but later decided to sell him as a slave to foreign merchants. He eventually was purchased by a wealthy government official. He was honest, hardworking and handsome. His master's wife had a crush on him and eventually began to make her moves on the young man. When she did not succeed, she accused him of raping her. Had the husband really believed his wife, he would have put the slave to death. However, he sent him to prison. The young man was gifted and had the powers to interpret dreams. Two prisoners had dreams and called on the young man's wisdom for interpretation. His interpretations turned out to be true. He had asked one of the dreamers to remember him when his dream came true. However, the man forgot him.

Why is it that we often forget those who bless us on our journey of life? None of us is self-made. We need one another. To forget to invest back in the communities and people that help us achieve our hopes and dreams is a path to a land where the unhappy, selfish and self-serving reside. However, those who invest back into the life of the community shine brighter than the sun.

Oprah Winfrey: I am impressed by an American business and entertainment icon – Oprah Winfrey. According to MSN, Ancestry.com report, August 9, 2004, Oprah was born in Kosciusko, Mississippi on January 29, 1954. "Oprah's mother Vernita Lee worked as a housemaid. Oprah's father Vernon Winfrey was serving in the armed forces. Vernita was 18 when Oprah was born and Vernon was 22. According to the report, a misprint on Oprah's birth certificate led to her famous first name. Her name was supposed to have been spelled 'Orpah' in reference to a biblical figure from the book of Ruth." The report further stated that because her parents were young and unmarried, Oprah was raised by her maternal grandmother Hattie Mae Lee. Her family was mainly agricultural. In the early census data, both sides of her family listed their profession as farmers.

Oprah Winfrey is one of the most celebrated and honored entertainers and business women in America and perhaps around the globe. I have been deeply touched by the fact that in spite of ranking among the wealthy "Who's Who," she has not forgotten the little people.

According to People News, Tuesday, November 23, 2004, 8:00 a.m. EST (reported by Todd Peterson), "Christmas came early for a studio audience of 300 schoolteachers and educators during a special taping of "The Oprah Winfrey Show." At the show that was taped "The teachers were delighted to learn they were the recipients of the annual 'Oprah's Favorite Things' – this year a $4.5 million giveaway that gives back to a deserving group." Audience members received gifts totally about $15,000 per person. This gift was three times the gift she had bestowed on people last year. "You give and give, and that is why I wanted to give you the hottest ticket in television," said Oprah to teachers. At the beginning of 2004, Oprah had demonstrated her generosity by giving keys to a brand new Pontiac G6 to 270 of her talk show attendees. When Oprah moves on to her sunset years, and one day she surely will, millions will remember her as the generous person who made their world a better place to live.

SOMETHING TO THINK ABOUT

Find a person you admire and study how they give back to the community. Some can give money, while others can give themselves and their time. What is your gift to the world?

Help Celebrate Christmas in April

MY DAUGHTER, MISTY, has taught me that it does not have to be December before we help someone celebrate Christmas. She has a real soft heart, the trait she has inherited from my wife. When Misty was in high school, mothers of students in her class would often call her for consultation to organize parties for their son or daughter. At times we would find out that a classmate had lost a parent and no one was going to take an interest in making his/her birthday a special event. So Misty would help organize a party for such a classmate. Making other people feel special, especially those who may be hurting, has been one of Misty's special talents. I admire young people who put others first, especially these days, when many young people can barely decide whether they should go to Wendy's or Jack-in-the-Box for lunch.

On December 11, 2004, I attended a program that featured high school students from Loma Linda California. They reported on their community service trip to Mexico where they helped with construction at an orphanage. The teacher who coordinated the service-learning project reported that in one day, students poured over 2,900 square yards of concrete. They showed a brief video of students in action. It was inspiring to see young people literally running and cheerfully carrying cement in wheelbarrows, moving dirt, and digging trenches. The students put big smiles on the faces of the orphans. These students helped the orphans celebrate Christmas during their Spring Break.

Several years ago, at my Rotary Club in Bakersfield, California, I was introduced to an agency called, "Christmas in April." Throughout the year, this organization partners with civic clubs and businesses to help build homes or shelters for those who may not be as blessed as the rest of us. Men and women from various businesses volunteer to work over the weekends, evenings and holidays to help poor people celebrate "Christmas" regardless of the time of the year.

When I was still with the government in the field of public health in Kern County, California, government leaders developed a novel approach to address the needs of disadvantaged communities. They develop the concept of "Neighborhood Partnerships." The entire County was divided into regional partnerships. Government, public and private service agencies pooled resources, studied community needs, set priorities and allocated resources to help people celebrate "Christmas" throughout the year. This was an innovative idea that caught fire and was subsequently adopted by other counties in California. If we are willing to sacrifice self and build on the "WE" power, we can help many people around us celebrate Christmas in April!

How do you celebrate Christmas? Do you wait for December 25 to show love and kindness? Do you tend to give gifts to members of your own family or children of your close friends? Many times we give gifts to people who don't even need a needle. True Christmas celebration is to put a smile on some lonely face and help the poor, widows, orphans and needy souls when they least expect it. Celebrate Christmas daily; who knows if you would see December 25 or not! Put a smile on the first sad face you see today; who knows if you would ever see that person again! May your journey of life be filled with generosity and songs of joy.

SOMETHING TO THINK ABOUT

What are your plans to help someone celebrate Christmas in April?

What blessings will you receive if you help others celebrate Christmas in April?

Don't Let the Chain of Love End With You

IN "BUILDING A Better You," you must start a random chain of love and keep it going. The world needs love. There is a place in every heart that only love can fill. The void in our own heart is filled best when we shower love on another lonely and needy heart. People can be rich and famous and yet lonely and sad. People have many ways to show their love. For example:

J. Leno, while interviewing Michael Douglas once related an interesting story about a gambler in Las Vegas. This man had a million dollars. He was playing $100,000 a hand. He called the waitress and asked her to get him a bottle of coke. When the waitress delivered the coke, the man asked her how much did she owe on her mortgage. The woman replied that she owed $40,000. He gave her a chip worth $40,000 and told her to go pay her mortgage.

George Martin, an attorney in Bakersfield, California, once related a heart warming and funny story. He told of a family that had taken their 19 year old daughter to La Vegas. Parents had checked into their room earlier. A few minutes later the girl took the elevator to join the parents. As soon as she got into the elevator, four big black men joined her. She was scared and stood frozen. One of the men finally said, "Lady, hit the floor." She quickly fell to the floor and lay flat. "I mean the floor you want to get off on," said the man. She slowly got up and hit the button and the elevator started.

Next day, she was still scared but ashamed that she misunderstood the man. Finally, a call came from the reception desk informing her that there was an envelope for her. She went down and discovered a note in it that read, "I am sorry that last night my bodyguards frightened you. To make it up to you, I have paid for your stay at the hotel." It was signed by Lionel Ritchie. This world is full of generous people who are sharing their love randomly.

In Bakersfield, California, my friends Jimmy Wei and his wife Dianna started a program called, "Meet and Eat." Jimmy is #1 Chef. He can cook food of any country in the world. Every Tuesday, Jimmy takes off from his hospital work and prepares a feast that would make Martha Stewart proud of him. Anyone is invited. People of all walks of life come together and share ways to bless the little corner of the world within their reach.

On December 13, 2004, KNX Radio did a feature in which they read letters to Santa from children. I wept listening to the heart-touching letters. One child asked Santa for a box of matches so they can light a fire in their mobile home because it is very cold. Another child told Santa "Our father does not want us any more. My mother works very hard on three jobs to take care of us. Please give something to my mom. She really needs it." None of the children asked for toys or things for themselves. This world is cold and needy, spread your love generously.

In their innocence, children reveal to us eternal principles of life. Let us be like little children, think beyond self, live by true priorities and find a purpose for living.

SOMETHING TO THINK ABOUT

Take a look around you and you will find sad and lonely people. Be proactive and look for opportunities to make the chain of love mend the broken hearts around you.

Chain of Love

(Album Live Laugh Love by Clay Walker)

He was driving home one evening,
In his beat up Pontiac
When an old lady flagged him down,
Her Mercedes had a flat
He could see that she was frightened,
Standing out there in the snow
'til he said I'm here to help you ma'am,
By the way, my name is Joe

She said I'm from St. Louis,
And I'm only passing through
I must have seen a hundred cars go by,
This is awful nice of you
When he changed the tire,
And closed her trunk
And was about to drive away,
She said how much do I owe you
Here's what he had to say

You don't owe me a thing, I've been there too
Someone once helped me out,
Just the way I'm helping you
If you really want to pay me back,
Here's what you do
Don't let the chain of love end with you
Well a few miles down the road,
The lady saw a small cafe
She went in to grab a bite to eat,

And then be on her way
But she couldn't help but notice,
How the waitress smiled so sweet
And how she must've been eight months
along, And dead on her feet
And though she didn't know her story,
And she probably never will
When the waitress went to get her change,
From a hundred dollar bill
The lady slipped right out the door,
And on a napkin left a note
There were tears in the waitress's eyes,
When she read what she wrote

You don't owe me a thing,
I've been there too
Someone once helped me out,
Just the way I'm helping you
If you really want to pay me back,
Here's what you do
Don't let the chain of love end with you

That night when she got home from work,
The waitress climbed into bed
She was thinkin' about the money,
And what the lady's note had said
As her husband lay there sleeping,
She whispered soft and low
Everything's gonna be alright, I love you, Joe.

SOMETHING TO THINK ABOUT

Think about people who have been good to you. Think about the generosity others have shown to you on your journey of life. I can think of hundreds of experiences where some kind soul appeared unexpectedly to ensure that I would have a safe passage. While we can never repay those who blessed us, we can certainly honor them by perpetuating the chain of love. At a time when this world is giving birth to more and more members of the "Me Generation," those who have their minds realigned, have an obligation to revive the soul of humanity to kindle the spirit of unity in the community.

Don't Be a Stinking Guest

T HERE IS AN old saying, "Guests and fish begin to stink after three days." We love guests. In fact, for the first thirteen years of our married life, we always had someone living with us who were simply passing through tough valleys of his/her life – friends, relatives and strangers in need of temporary hospitality. My wife has an extra special gift for making people feel comfortable and welcome. During our first year of marriage, we entertained over 300 guests for lunch or dinner. We are not necessarily the social type. We may have been invited by no more than thirty of these individuals. We just love company. We have been greatly blessed by the company of most of our guests. However, some guests have tested our patience.

Once a couple was renovating their house and asked to live with one of our friends. The couple was adorable but inseparable from their big extra-active dog. Our friends had a picture-perfect lawn. In no time the lawn had patches of yellow. To add to the situation, the young lady was so free-spirited that she left the lights on in every room she visited and especially kept the door open between the garage and the house with air-conditioner running. The host family blessed the Edison Company a lot more than their usual share during the time the guests stayed with them. The same couple wanted to stay with them again. To everyone's surprise, the lady said, "Wherever we live, our dog lives." Our friends had to politely reply that the former guests might have to live wherever the dog was going to live, because the dog would not be living here."

Once a father brought his four-year old child to our home. The child was jumping all over our furniture with shoes and poking holes in my Sansui speakers. When I tried to stop the boy from ruining my speakers, the father replied, "I allow him to do that at my house." I could not believe my ears. I quickly responded, "But this is not your home." He quickly picked up the boy and left, promising never to visit us again. Then we had another guest who heard my wife and me expressing our difference of opinions on a topic. He concluded that we were headed for a divorce and tried to be a marriage counselor. Another time a guest took the responsibility of administering corporal punishment to our little son. However, we have entertained many guests who have greatly enriched our lives. Oh, how we wish they would visit us more often!

We had one guest who had a habit of getting up very early. By the time we would get up, she would have cleaned up the kitchen and even fixed breakfast and sometimes even dinner for us. She was just like a member of the family. If she would go shopping, she would come home with groceries or some special gift for the family. I can share memories of many guests who greatly blessed our home and made the journey of life much lighter. **See next page for tips on becoming a welcome guest.**

SOMETHING TO THINK ABOUT

Write down ten ways you can bless the hostess if you are a guest in someone's home.

What do you think people say about you as their guest when you leave their home?

Tips on Becoming a Welcome Guest

SOONER OR LATER you will be a guest in someone's home. You want to leave the host family wishing you could stay longer, come more often, bless their home and enrich their lives. If the children of the host family fall in love with you, you will find parents becoming your admirers and looking forward to your next visit. Here are a few suggestions. If kept in mind, they may make a big difference between helping you become a welcome visitor or prompting the host to whisper as you leave, "Good riddance."

- Be a low maintenance guest. Reduce the use of anything that would cost the host money.

- Don't discuss political parties or religion – you may find the host on the opposite side.

- Be prepared to take the host family for dinner to lighten their burden for keeping you.

- If you make local calls, keep them **VERY** brief, better yet, use your own cell phone.

- Don't ask the host to buy special food for you. Give thanks and eat what they offer.

- Don't give the host family medical advice. They have a family doctor for that.

- Don't borrow their car. If you do, have it cleaned and filled before returning.

- If you invite guests for meals, take the host and the guests to a restaurant.

- Don't criticize others when you are a guest – the host could be related.

- Don't try to discipline their children – you are not their social worker.

- Don't ever intervene when the parents are correcting their children.

- Don't tell the host family what to do – you are not their supervisor.

- Offer to help in the kitchen, unless it is against the host's culture.

- Don't give the family advice – you are a guest not a counselor.

- Don't invite friends for meals unless you check with the host.

- Clean up after yourself. The host is not your maid or servant.

- Don't insist on watching your favorite show or news.

- Make your own bed and keep your bathroom clean.

- When on the telephone, keep your voice down.

- Bring a gift for a child or the lady of the house.

- Do your own laundry or take it to the cleaners.

- Don't ask the host to run errands for you.

- Don't park in the driveway unless asked.

- Don't stay up late to watch movies.

SOMETHING TO THINK ABOUT

Think of the guest you would not want to entertain again and make a list of your reasons.

Think of fifteen things you can do to become a Welcome Guest.

Write a letter to thank people who have entertained you as a guest.

Be a Collector – Not a "Pack-rat" (Part I)

WHEN I WAS in graduate school, a kind elderly lady offered me free lodging in exchange for my caring for her yard. One day she asked me to help her clean her garage. After nine hours of work in the cold, I grew twenty years older and had a splitting headache by the end of the day, and yet nothing to show for progress. During her seventy-six years, she had gathered so much "junk" (treasures according to her) that I was not allowed to throw away a single thing. All I did was to rearrange the place. Every now and then she would say, "I have had that for fifty years. Who knows I may need it later." I am sure this story sounds familiar. I quickly concluded that she was a "Pack-Rat."

I love to see art work. I admire those who invest in collecting valuable art to preserve history and culture for future generations. On your journey of life, you will encounter many things, some will serve you better if discarded, and some will prove to be invaluable if you tend to them. Let me suggest a few things you may want to collect to enrich your life and future.

COLLECT PLEASANT MEMORIES: Take an inventory of your life and collect as many pleasant memories as you can. These memories will help you get over the hump in case someone throws some lemons in your direction. These memories will keep you going when going gets tough.

COLLECT NAMES OF GOOD SAMARITANS: Good Samaritans are good friends. They are better than medicine. It takes time to build healthy friendships. Keep in touch with your friends. They are like legs of your table. If you keep losing them one by one, eventually you will have no leg to stand on. On our journey, there are bumps and bruises and, interestingly, there is always a Good Samaritan who shows up unexpectedly to our rescue. Send them a note of appreciation, at least once a year. Like old wine, if nurtured, friendships should become stronger and more endearing over the years.

COLLECT GOOD BOOKS, TAPES AND VIDEOS: Good books, videos and tapes are like your favorite friends and teachers. They can cut short your learning curve so YOU don't have to make all the mistakes to get your life in order. Stay hungry and teachable.

MAKE A LIST OF HARD TIMES THAT MADE YOU STRONGER AND WISER: Don't forget the tough experiences that made you stronger and better equipped to face challenges of life. They help you realize that there is life after a failure. If you are reading this book, you already know that people who slighted you were not able to keep you down, the rainy days did not last, the missed opportunities did not mean the end of the world, your heart kept on beating in spite of all the heartbreaks and heartaches, and all those bumps and bruises eventually healed. You have discovered that you are resilient and resourceful. Unless you intentionally give up on yourself, no one and nothing can defeat you. You are invincible. You were born to win because you can. You were not born to be poor, sick or miserable. You were born to enjoy life and enjoy it abundantly. So, go and live your life to the fullest.

SOMETHING TO THINK ABOUT

Purchase a special album and develop a "BOOK OF GOOD MEMORIES."

Be a Collector – Not a "Pack-rat" (Part II)

REMEMBER SPECIAL EVENTS AND DAYS: There are days and events that have special significance for each family, such as, wedding anniversary, birthdays, child's first step, your baby's first word, and so on. It is not prudent to forget such days. When my children were in grade school, I was so grateful to their teachers who kept track of "Mother's Day, Father's Day," etc. These days and events tell the family and friends that you really care about them and that they are on your mind. People like to hear that someone is thinking of them.

REMEMBER HOW YOU FELT WHEN YOU SAW YOUR NEWBORN BABY: When my son was born I was holding him in my arms and jumping all over the delivery room shouting, "It's a Boy, It's a Boy." I was so excited that the nurses felt I had gone out of my mind. I had the same excitement when my daughter was born. Seeing a newborn baby gives me so much hope for the future. It reminds me that humans can have a new beginning. We are the only animals who can put a lid over the past unpleasant experiences and start over. Do you have the wisdom to start over without chaining yourself to the past? It is hard to move forward while facing backward!

COLLECT SPECIAL RECIPIES: Before I got married, I visited my would-be in-laws. My would-be wife tried so hard to teach me how to fry an egg. I had finished college and I was already working for a couple of years. I was staying by myself and cooking had became a real necessity. However, I did not let my would-be wife know about my hidden "cooking skills." I listened to her describe her egg-frying recipe with great delight. I still remember the entire scene. It is very special to me because it showed that she cared enough to impart her knowledge. The family had a good laugh watching my intense interest in her first cooking lesson. It still brings good memories to my mind. Maybe you have a recipe your spouse used to prepare the first meal for you after the wedding. May be your child tried to teach you how to make pancakes when he/she was five years old. Maybe it's your Grandma's favorite recipe!

MAKE A LIST OF SONGS THAT MADE YOU DANCE WITH ROMANCE: Think of the song they played at your prom, first date, wedding day, at your honeymoon, and so on. If it made you dance then, why not take the time to relive the beginning of your romance. Who knows, you may rekindle the fire and bring life to your relationship. Music has a way of bringing back good memories to renew our soul. What song puts a smile on your face? Keep a song in your heart.

SOMETHING TO THINK ABOUT

If you find yourself falling out of love with your spouse or taking your life for granted, you can go back to your "Book of Good Memories," and ignite the fire to warm up your lonely and worn out spirit. It is so easy to fall into the rut and the mundane. However, life is so exciting. Don't let the clouds hide your rainbow. Nature has a lot to teach us. For example, the sun never sets. It does not move. It holds its ground and keeps shining behind the thick clouds, fog, smog, and dense darkness. When faced with doom and gloom, picture yourself as the sun. When drenched in the rain, remember the sunny days.

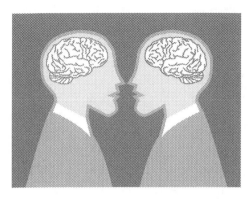

Healing Your
Feelings (Part I)

I CAN IDENTIFY with the old Negro Spiritual – "Sometimes, I feel like a motherless child, far away from home..." Feelings are like ghosts. They don't have to have any grounds to chase you and yet they hound you day and night, even when you are asleep. Feelings may be based on imaginary experiences but they have rock-solid impact on the way we live and behave. You can be physically healthy as a horse, and yet driven nuts by your bad feelings. They play hide and seek to torment you and make you sweat. If I could get inside your mind, I would see a bumper crop of feelings, some laying land mines to trip you on your journey of life. During my three years of work in drug abuse prevention education and counseling at California Youth Authority facilities, I heard youth express feelings that made my stomach churn. Let me share some of these feelings with you that the youth shared with me.

"Sometimes I feel like I am stranded in the desert with 120 degree heat in shade and not a drop of water. Sometimes I feel like a little chicken being pursued by 1000 wolves. Sometimes I feel I am hanging mid-air with a thin rope about to snap, and as I look down, I see a large pit with a million cobras anxious to welcome their prey. Sometimes I feel like one of the five children of Andrea Yates (The Texas baby killer), comforted only by my ignorance of the impending doom that awaits me. Sometimes I feel lost in the jungle, abandoned and no hope of being rescued."

"Sometimes I feel that I am just an unknown and lonely face among a sea of young, successful trendy people who are too busy to see the pain on my face. Sometimes I feel like a man with a broken heart, shattered dreams, an aborted mission, and it seems like I have come to the end of my road, and I have wasted all my opportunities to make a difference on this earth. Sometimes I feel like a person who has been tuned to the bad news radio so long that my ear drums are busted and I can no longer hear the good news. It seems that hope has faded, leaving me in the valley where just gloom and doom encircle me."

"Sometimes I feel like a farmer who is sitting at the edge of his farm holding, his head in his hands and weeping bitterly, because it is harvest time and weeds have choked his crop.

Sometimes I feel like a man waiting at the airport with a bouquet of five dozen long-stem red roses, but no one to receive them from me. Sometimes I feel like a book with the last chapter featuring the bitter end of the hero. Sometimes I feel like the clouds without the rain, rainbow with only the blue color, and a fig tree with plenty of leaves but no fruit. Sometimes I have sat at the edge of a cliff and the distance between despair and hope has been wider than the distance between the north and south rims of Grand Canyon. There have been times when I have felt that my life has been just one big bad dream. Sometimes I feel that my life is a complicated puzzle, and I cannot find the missing pieces. Sometimes when I am laying in my bed I feel my world is crowding in on me." Can you identify with these young people? You may not be able to control such feelings but you can certainly choose how to respond.

According to the US News report, May 30, 2008, "The number of Army suicides in 2007 increased by 13% over 2006. As the family system continues to deteriorate in America, teen suicides have been on the rise. According to some estimates, one in five Americans can benefit from psychological counseling. On next page, I have presented tips on coping with despair.

SOMETHING TO THINK ABOUT

Write down your feelings as truthfully as you can. What do you generally do with such feelings?

Healing Your Feelings (Part II)

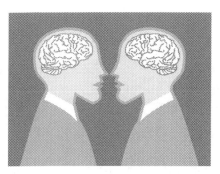

HAVE YOU EVER been plagued by bad feelings such as described in the previous chapter? I wish I could tell you that you are the only one, but that would not be true. It is normal to have such feelings; however, to dwell on them and allow them to affect your mind will hold you hostage and lead you to the valley of self-destruction. Feelings are like the clouds, they come and they disappear. Charting your course by the way you feel is like building your castles in the sand. Feelings are often affected by external cues. Our judgment is often blurred when we are moved to action only by our feelings. Feelings can be triggered by a single incident. However, to deal with feelings effectively, one must keep focused on the big picture and see life in its total reality.

Here are a few recommendations to help you spot the rainbow when you are loaded with a barrel of bad feelings and passing through the dark valley:

Watch the movie "Gandhi" and learn the true purpose of life.

Visit a neighbor who has lost a loved one and comfort him/her.

Watch the children at play and see them make up after the fight.

Learn from a couple that has just annulled their ten year marriage.

Look up to the sky after the rain – and admire the rainbow colors.

Go bird watching and observe the sparrows sing and dance carefree.

Watch the cactus plants in the desert - how do you think they bloom?

Visit the elderly in a convalescent home and discover the value of life.

Spend a day at a homeless shelter and discover how fortunate you are.

Read the life of Nelson Mandela and learn the true struggle for justice.

Review the past ten years of your life and discover your survival skills.

Watch a toddler and learn the art of starting
over and over and over again.

Visit a widow who has sacrificed her husband
in the defense of the country.

Study the life of Helen Keller and discover
the value of vision over eyesight.

Visit the Sequoia National Forest and ask the trees
how they weather the bitter storms.

Watch the rich, the famous and the powerful and
see their pain in spite of fat bank accounts.

Sit by the waters, walk through the woods, pick some
wild flowers, and look inside your soul.

SOMETHING TO THINK ABOUT

If life were pain-free there would be no newborn babies. If the seed did not die, it would mark the end of life. If there were no fall season, how would you recognize the spring? If there were no winter, would you know the importance of summer? Struggle is the price we pay for freedom.

Be Kind to
the Elderly

B ETTE MIDLER IN one of her songs conveys one of the most powerful life changing messages, "…You know that old trees just grow stronger, and old rivers grow wilder every day, but old people, they just grow lonesome waiting for someone to say, 'Hello in there. Hello.'" She then advises, "So if you're walking down the street sometime and you should spot some hollow ancient eyes, don't you pass them by and stare as if you didn't care. Say, 'Hello in there. Hello.'"

One of my special hobbies is to visit the elderly folks in convalescent homes or other shut-in facilities. I remember once I was visiting an elderly woman in a hospital. As I smiled and said hello, she quickly grabbed my hand and held it tightly. "I knew you would be coming. Shall I tell you what I do for my entertainment?" she asked. "Please tell me, I want to know," I said. "I dial the telephone and listen to the dial tone," she replied. My heart just sank within me. I began to imagine what an active person she must have been when she was young. Another elderly woman told me about her love for driving. "I used to go from Loma Linda, California to San Francisco in five hours." It takes me almost eight hours to travel that distance and she could do it in five! I knew instantly that I was face-to-face with a woman who once was a mover and shaker in her circles. Now, here she is in a hospital bed, living on her past as the future was slipping away from her rapidly.

Once I asked permission to conduct an observational study of elderly clients who were being treated at a physical therapy department of a large medical center. A physical therapist was frustrated with an elderly man. She wanted him to take off all his clothes so she could give him a bath.

The client almost choked her for asking him to undress. I offered to assist her. The patient had suffered a stroke and could not speak. I met with the family and learned that the patient used to be a very conservative church leader. In his times, holding hands prior to marriage was being lustful. He held high moral values and respected women. He was not about to take his clothes off in front of a young girl. I suggested that a male therapist be assigned to the patient and that the patient should be asked to keep his shorts on for bathing. The client complied happily. Know the story behind the face. See the elderly the way they were in the prime of their life. Treat them like people who can teach you a few things about life, its value and purpose.

Grandmothers on both sides of my family died at age 102 and 103. Both of them lived independently, worked until the day they died, and took pride that they did not need help from others to manage their daily chores. People in their eighties these days are bungee-jumping, hang-gliding and riding motorcycles. Don't stereotype. Look behind the hollow eyes. Each elderly person is a treasure-chest of information, knowledge and wisdom. The elderly can help the young link to their past, discover the value of the present and lay a strong foundation for a brighter future. Ignoring the elderly is to walk blindfolded into the future.

Don't let this catch you by surprise that we who think of ourselves as young, strong and healthy will also someday become old, feeble and a mere memory in the minds of the new generation. How will the new generation treat us when we get there? Just as we treat the elderly among us. By respecting the elderly we can be the recipients of wisdom that money cannot buy.

SOMETHING TO THINK ABOUT

Do you read the story when you see an elderly face? Do you see an opportunity to link to the past and learn? What's in a face? There is a rich story behind each face to enrich your life.

Be Kind to the Elderly

"Hello in There"

We had an apartment in the city. I and my husband liked living there.

It's been years since the kids have grown, a
life of their own, left us alone.

John and Linda live in Omaha.

Joe is somewhere on the road.

We lost Davy in the Korean war.

I still don't know what for, don't matter any more.

You know that old trees just grow stronger,

and old rivers grow wilder every day,

but old people, they just grow lonesome

waiting for someone to say,

"Hello in there. Hello"

Me and my husband, we don't talk much anymore.

He sits and stares through the backdoor screen.

And all the news just repeats itself

like some forgotten dream

that we've both seen.

Someday I'll go and call up Judy.

We worked together at the factory.

Ah, but what would I say when she asks what's new?

Say, "Nothing, what's with you?

Nothing much to do."

Old trees just grow stronger,

and old rivers grow wilder every day,

Ah, but, but old people, they just grow lonesome

waiting for someone to say,

"Hello in There. Hello."

So if you're walking down the street sometime

and you should spot some hollow ancient eyes,

don't you pass them by and stare

as if you didn't care.

Say, "Hello in there. Hello."

HELLO IN THERE

JOHN PRINE

© 1971 WALDEN MUSIC, INC. & SOUR GRAPES MUSIC

All rights on behalf of WALDEN MUSIC, INC. Administered by WB MUSIC CORP.

All Rights Reserved. Used by permission from ALFRED PUBLISHING CO., INC

Be a Stress Buster Follow a Stress Buster's Creed

JUST LIVING ON this planet is a challenge; however, I would not exchange it for the alternative, even if someone paid me a million dollars. You have no idea how many people walk around with a plastic smile and a big hole in their head or heart. Some people around you are merely "Walking Dead," while others are simply trying to get by. Many of them are scared to go home and face their demons. If we really knew what people may be going through, we probably would shower flowers to cheer them up and be grateful for our blessings. Become a Stress Buster not a stress carrier. Build good relationships with people. Follow this creed and make someone's day!

I WILL THINK BEFORE I SPEAK.

I will not put my foot in my mouth.

I WILL SPEAK LESS AND LISTEN MORE.

I will let others impress me.

I WILL KEEP MY MIND OVER MY MOUTH.

The less I say, the less people will have to hold against me.

I WILL NOT INTERRUPT WHEN OTHERS ARE SPEAKING.

I will listen with my heart to understand others' point of view.

I WILL NOT TRY TO WIN AN ARGUMENT.

I know it is better to solve a problem than to win a debate.

I WILL NOT JUDGE, LEST I BE JUDGED;

I will first take the beam out of my own eye,

before pointing out a mote in someone else's eye.

WHEN SPEAKING, I WILL USE SOFT WORDS;

IN CASE I HAVE TO SWALLOW THEM.

I WILL PUT OTHERS FIRST.

I will make any excuse to be of service

to others and enrich my soul.

I WILL COMMUNICATE DIRECTLY.

I will not gossip. I will talk to people rather than about them.

I WILL FORGIVE WITHOUT BEING ASKED.

People need us because of their weaknesses, not their strengths.

Tsunamis: Test Your Will to Unite

ACCORDING TO THE Associated Press report, December 27, 12:20 p.m., ET, "A tsunami is a series of traveling ocean waves generated by geological disturbances near the ocean floor. With nothing to stop them, the waves can race across the ocean like the crack of a bullwhip, gaining momentum over thousands of miles." According to the U.S. Geological Survey, a 9.0 magnitude temblor, the strongest in four decades, hit southern Asia on Sunday, December 26, 2004, that set in motion the most powerful tsunamis that devastated a host of countries including: Bangladesh, India, Indonesia, Malaysia, Maldives, the Andaman and Nicobar islands, Myanmar, Sri Lanka, Seychelles, Thailand and even Somalia. According to the reports, "the waves sped away from the epicenter at over 500 miles per hour before crashing into the region's shorelines, sweeping people and fishing villages out to sea." Over 150,000 died and more than four millions were displaced from their homes and resort hotels. The Associated Press reported at 12:20 p.m. on December 27, 2004 that coastal "beaches became open-air mortuaries as fishermen's bodies washed ashore, and retreating waters left behind others killed inland." I watched big bulldozers moving mangled and twisted dead bodies like they were moving dirt around a construction site. Thousands of people were injured. I had never seen disaster of this magnitude in my entire life. Never had I witnessed nature attacking humans with such brutal force without warning.

It appeared as though the angry earth and water teamed up to attack human beings without warning, giving not even a few seconds for people to arm themselves. The water rushed with a roar and then suddenly retreated. It was reported that over forty feet high waves came right back to kill and demolish everything in their path, including all man-made resort facilities, homes of the rich and famous along with shacks of the lowly people.

According to the Associated Press, December 28, 5:55 p.m. ET, 2004, "A German statesman, a Czech supermodel and a Swedish Olympic ski champion were among the vacationers whose search for peace and sun in tropical southern Asia was shattered by the tsunamis that spared neither rich nor poor." Former German Chancellor Helmut Kohl was on holiday in Sri Lanka. The helicopter was able to rescue him and his family. However, there were thousands of others who were not so fortunate. Hollywood actor-director Richard Attenborough who directed the movie Gandhi also suffered loss. His granddaughter Lucy, 14, perished and his daughter, Jane and her mother-in-law were missing in Phuket resort in Thailand. Thailand's royal family lost Thai-American grandson of King Phumipol Adulyadej, Poom Jensen, 21, who was jet skiing when the tidal wave struck Phuket.

The forces of nature were at war with humans and the humans found themselves unprepared and powerless. Nature attacked with vengeance to test the human will to unite and fight for one another's survival. It personally delivered a message with the sound of thunder that it does not respect the differences we make between the rich, poor, black, white, the powerful and the humble. Did you hear it?

SOMETHING TO THINK ABOUT

Unless the human family unites, its members will perish while pampering their pride and individuality.

What steps would you take to create unity in your family, at your work place and in your community?

RECCOMMENDATIONS TO CREATE UNITY

_____

_____

_____

_____

_____

_____

_____

_____

_____

_____

_____

_____

_____

_____

_____

_____

_____

_____

_____

Human Response to Nature's Call for Unity

(Photo – Getty Images – Used with permission)

ACCORDING TO THE Red Cross, "It was feared the death toll in Sunday's earthquake and tsunamis in the Indian Ocean could top 150,000." According to the Associated Press "An international tsunami warning system was started in 1965, after the Alaska quake, designed to advise coastal communities of a potentially killer wave. Member states include all the major Pacific rim nations in North America, Asia and South America. But because tsunamis are rare in the Indian Ocean, India and Sri Lanka were not part of the system." The report further stated that scientists believe that the death toll would have been reduced if India and Sri Lanka had been members of the international tsunami warning system. With an underground activity of the magnitude generated by earthquake, one wonders how the international tsunami warning scientists failed to detect such an event! (Internet report by NBC News and other media at 9:49 a.m. EST on December 29, 2004).

According to NBC report, 9:49 a.m. EST December 29, 2004, this event was of unprecedented magnitude. "We have little hope, except for individual miracles," Chairman Jean-Marc Espalioux of the Accor hotel group said of the search for thousands of tourists and locals missing from beach resorts of southern Thailand." Millions were made homeless. Threat of hunger and disease made United Nations and World Health Organization (WHO) call upon the world to unite to face the challenge.

Dr. David Nabarro, head of crisis operations for the WHO said, "The initial terror associated with the tsunamis and the earthquake itself may be dwarfed by the longer-term suffering of the affected communities."

Events of this magnitude remind us that our world is a one big global village. We are connected and our survival depends on putting our differences aside and embracing the principle of one universal family. As a group, we may at times lose a battle against natural forces, but we will not be defeated. Our spirit will never be broken. Such global disasters demonstrate our national character, our belief about our role in the world, our national priorities and our vision for the future. The character of a nation is built upon the character of its states, cities, communities, neighborhoods and families. Ultimately, the character of a nation is shaped by the life and character of each one of its sons and daughters. Can your nation depend on you for building and demonstrating its character at its best at times of local, national or international disasters? Can your neighborhood depend on you as its guardian?

It is a general tendency for one to think of himself/herself as a self-contained and independent unit, needing nothing from others and feeling no need to contribute to the preservation of the group. However, when hit by personal tsunamis, we quickly recognize that we are part of a much bigger picture and that survival of each one of us is tied with the survival of our reference group. In isolation and inflated sense of self-sufficiency, we begin to shrink, and ultimately die, thus aborting our hopes and dreams. For whatever reason, in the face of tragedy, there is a hidden resolve among nations to unite and fight for survival. We have a kinship that seems to come alive only at a time of calamity.

SOMETHING TO THINK ABOUT

What is your plan to retool your mind to demonstrate oneness with all mankind?

Facing the Tsunamis: The Resilient Human Spirit

HUMAN BEINGS ARE resilient. The U.S. State Department published a list of 43 organizations that were accepting donations in America alone to help the victims of the 9.0 magnitude earthquake that shook southern Asia and provided momentum to 500 mph and 30-40 feet high tsunamis on Sunday, December 26, 2004. Within a few days, countries from around the world pledged $2 billion for the victims of the disaster.

Additionally, national and international relief agencies and government organizations were hard at work to coordinate resources to reach the needy in the affected regions of the world. Schools, universities, churches and civic clubs around the world were leaving no stone unturned to appeal to their members to reach out to the victims both financially and by praying for comfort and hope for those who have suffered irreparable loss. People of all ages, professionals with all types of specialties and talents were volunteering to go to the ravaged areas and help. CNN featured a two- hour special report, "Anderson Cooper 360" on December 29, 2004, 10-12 p.m. They reported on a 14 year old boy who had set up a website to collect donations to send to the victims.

According to the Associated Press, December 30, 8:02 a.m. ET, The United States diverted several warships and helicopters to the earthquake-ravaged regions. Ships provided millions of gallons of fresh drinking water each day, while helicopters distributed food and relief supplies to remote areas. World powers declared a debt-repayment moratorium to relieve the financial burden on victim nations. President George W. Bush requested his father, former president George Bush Sr. and his one-time rival, former president William Jefferson Clinton, to head up a national fund raising drive to help the tsunami victims.

Celebrities, athletes, royalties and poor, all gave something to relieve suffering. People from around the world donated food, clothes, money and even their own blood to care for the injured in hospitals and clinics. United, humanity has overcome the ravages of two world wars, a host of tribal genocides and 9/11 in the U.S. Our unified resolve will serve as a reminder of nature's brutal attack and how it prompted humanity to unite its global family. The question that plagued me during this ordeal was "Why does it take a disaster for us to realize that we are one big human family and that the survival of any one of us is linked with the survival of all of us?

According to CNN, terrorists attacked ten sites in Mumbai, India on Wednesday, November 26, 2008. The two luxury hotels, Taj Mahal and Obroi, the main train station and a Jewish center Chabad House were among the targets. About 200 people were killed by the gunmen and nearly 300 wounded. There were six Americans among the victims. The global nature of the terror invoked unity among the peace loving nations of the world. If nations were to unite and work together in time of peace, they would be better equipped to deal with the dissident elements at time of crisis. Our world has become a one big global village. We can no longer view events in isolation. To arrest evil, all nations must unite or face destruction and chaos one by one. All nations suffer when tragedy faced by one is forgotten or ignored. This tragedy also cost the Indian Home Minister Shivraj Patel his job (source: MSNBC).

SOMETHING TO THINK ABOUT

Do you believe that it is the disintegration of the family that is destroying our civilization?

Tsunamis' Gift to the World

IN MANY PARTS of the world, some people may view the unprecedented devastation as nature's way of getting the attention of humanity. Many people believe that "gods" that dwell beneath the earth were not pleased with what man was doing to mother earth. The "gods" were especially displeased how humans treat one another. The "gods" did not like the hatred and indifference, selfishness and self-serving behavior of humans. Thus, nature wanted to test our priorities and preoccupation. It wanted to test if we really cared for one another. Tsunamis have succeeded in awakening the spirit and conscience of the world and taught us several valuable lessons.

Life Is Temporary and Unpredictable.   When the tsunamis attacked, many who were sipping on their pina colada, eating their caviar or mending their fishing nets did not even have a second's warning to be ready for battle with nature. We **MUST** be ready at all times. Every second must be considered a special gift and invested in concluding the business at hand.

We Are All Part of One Family. If nature had any doubt about us, we have demonstrated that we are resilient. We are one big family in spite of our place of origin, economic status, place in society or our beliefs about politics, religion or life and death. We need one another. We must put our differences aside if we want to survive the tsunamis we face each day on our journey of life. We are organs of the same body. What affects one, affects the entire human race.

We Live In a Global Village. Let's not wait for tsunamis to unite us or show that we care for one another. At home, at work, in the market place or while we travel around the planet, we are barely at arm's length from where we started. The earthquake that devastated southern Asia will always serve as a vivid reminder that our destiny is linked and we need one another for survival.

Put Values Above Valuables. Watching the forty foot high angry waves sweep away every-thing in their path on Sunday, December 27, 2004, I became very cognizant that values must take higher priority over valuables. Instead of gathering goods that can be taken away in a moment, or building castles in the sand, we must build the people we live with and work with. A life lived with such priorities will have no regrets regardless of its length.

Don't Wait For Tsunamis to Hold Hands or Hug. MSNBC reported on December 27, 2004, 9:03 p.m. that California golf professional, William Robins was honeymooning with his bride, Amanda. When the waves hit, they thought it was a bomb. "We held hands and crouched in the corner. Then we heard a rumbling explosion that didn't end," said Robins. Later, when a concrete wall collapsed they were pushed through two layers of concrete and forced to let go of each other's hands, said Amanda, 27, who suffered a broken pelvis. "Our paradise turned into hell," said American tourist Moira Lee, 28, who was having coffee on Phuket's Patpong Beach. Foreign visitors in Sri Lanka were stunned by the hospitality of the locals. "They gave us the shirts they were wearing. They gave us their slippers. They are the most beautiful people in the world," said Jorg Dietrichs, one of four German backpackers taken in by a family after they were left with nothing but their swimming trunks.

SOMETHING TO THINK ABOUT

Let's live like one family so that when a disaster hits, we will be able to hold hands and stick together. While it is inconceivable that nations can live like one big happy family, such spirit can indeed live and thrive in the hearts of individuals.

Feel The Tide of Grief: Tragedy and Heroism?

(Photo- Getty Images, Used with Permission)

THIS PICTURE MAKES you shudder and clinch your teeth with grief. Even if I knew no one personally who became a human sacrifice to the raging sea, a little bit of me has also died with these victims. I will never be complete with them gone. They have taken a piece of me with them. I pictured myself in the place of the person standing in this photograph. The feelings that engulfed my soul can never be captured in words. To me each victim represents an unfinished dream, abrupt ending of a story, and a movie without the final scene.

On December 26, according to geologist Simon Winchester, author of "Krakatoa," a book about a volcano that exploded off Sumatra in 1883, killing 40,000 people, "The earth shrugged for a moment. Everything moved a little." (Source: Article by Evan Thomas and George Wehrfritz, Newsweek, 2:09 p.m. ET Jan, 2005, on the internet). He further stated that, "The quake jolted the Earth's rotation enough to trim a couple of microseconds off the clock." It seems that when the earth just winks, the mountains shake. The devastation shown in the picture above is accompanied by many heroic stories like the rescue of "Petra Nemcova, cover girl of the 2003 Sports Illustrated swimsuit issue, who clung to a tree for eight hours." Rescuers also found a 20 days old baby floating on a mattress, crying but alive.

One of the most fascinating stories is that of an elephant. According to a news report, a group of children were riding an elephant for fun. However, all of a sudden, the animal took off to the mountains. Parents, fearing that the animal may trample the children, ran after the elephant. Both the parents and the children were led to the safe ground by the elephant just before the tsunamis hit the area. Rescuers also noted that no animals were found dead as a result of tsunamis.

Do you suppose the animals have a" sixth" sense? Is it possible that animals are more in tune with mother earth and are able to communicate better with the forces of nature? Is it possible that the animals have a better kinship with one another and they have developed a joint tsunami, tornado or hurricane warning system? Do you suppose the sea animals can communicate with mammals on the ground and warn them of the impending doom? What if the "little bird" spread the word about tsunamis to all the creatures?

Advances in technology have linked even the remote unknown parts of the world to make this planet a one big global village. What happens in one corner of the world; can be seen instantly all over the world. We can pick up our ipod and transmit not just messages but images and feelings across the world. We have never been closer to one another in history as we are today and yet, we have never felt more isolated and lonely than we do today.

SOMETHNG TO THINK ABOUT

As part of human family, every time I see someone die, I feel I am losing a part of me. Every time I see someone winning and having a good time, a ray of hope springs in my soul and brightens my path of life. The tragedy created by tsunamis has vividly inscribed in my mind that we are one. We need each other. We can magnify one another's joy and lessen the pain.

Be Empowered by Lasting Values

(Photo – Getty Images, Used with permission)

ON JANUARY 5, 2005, U. S. Secretary of State Colin Powell toured the tsunami stricken area. Walking toward a makeshift tent hospital at Banda Aceh airport in Indonesia the Secretary said, "I've been in war and I've been a diplomat…but I've never seen anything like this." Seeing hundreds of volunteers and helicopters at work in helping the victims, the great diplomat agreed that true human values were at work. (Source: The Associated Press, 9:08 a.m. ET January 5, 2005). The fundamental human values transcended the religious and political ideologies and nations invested fiscal and human resources to help people of divergent political persuasions.

True Human Values Promote Life. Nations with true values invest endless resources to search and rescue a lost hiker, a lost crazy person, a stranded mountain climber, or even a cat up the flag pole. Even the enemies are accorded rights they never dreamed of in their own homeland.

True Human Values Promote Volunteerism and Philanthropy. Nations with true human values promote philanthropy and volunteerism to uplift humanity. In such nations schools, churches, civic organizations, governments and citizens work together to uplift the needy, and by doing so, they define the soul of a nation.

People with True Values Rescue and Rebuild. In Nations where true human values are nurtured, there is a history of burying the old hatchet and going to bat even for former enemies. The recent Tsunamis demonstrated in living colors how countries with drastically opposed ideologies came to rescue and rebuild the affected nations. Over the years, I have observed that when natural disasters strike, the true values and the character of nations come to life.

Many disaster victims were Muslims. At a time when the Western world was on edge because of the actions of the Muslim extremists in disrupting the world peace, the Western countries left no stone unturned to demonstrate that in spite of all ideological differences, civilized and freedom loving people all over the world felt oneness with their suffering brothers and sisters everywhere. My faith in human decency, courage and kinship was renewed, rejuvenated and restored. Let future generations, upon reading about these tragedies, learn that when nature tested and tried, the human spirit triumphed and transcended all barriers to unite.

Let every statesman around the world ensure that schools and synagogues all proclaim that love is better than hate, hope is more reassuring than despair, peace is more desirable than war, and unity is more powerful than living in isolation in oppressive and repressive systems.

I find it very revealing to assess my own lasting human values by asking myself questions: Do I promote life through all my dealings with people? Do I send a clear signal that I am not the center of the universe? Is the ultimate purpose of my life to look out for myself or to lend a helping hand to help others live a more productive life? Do I volunteer and give myself and my means to show my gratitude for the privilege to share a corner of this earth?

SOMETHING TO THINK ABOUT

Do my actions demonstrate that I will do my part to rescue and rebuild the broken-hearted, the lonely, the rejected, the friendless and even a foe?

Quit Griping and Enjoy the Good Life

ON JANUARY 7, 2005, 12:03 p.m. ET, The Associated Press reported on the climbing death toll due to the tsunami and featured this picture, showing a woman carrying her household belongings and covering her nose to guard herself from the "stench of decaying bodies" in Banda Aceh, Sumatra, Indonesia. In the picture were also seen the rescue workers in yellow jackets. On January 17, KNX 1070 radio station reported that the death toll had risen to 175,000 with untold numbers of people still missing.

During the week of tsunamis, December 26 – 30, 2004, everyone I met seemed very grateful for being alive. It almost seemed that there was a new appreciation for life and all its gifts. People were expressing their love for those around them through letters, e-mails and telephone calls. People seemed to appreciate food, clothing, shelter, clean drinking water, clean air, being surrounded by their loved ones, and being in a country far from any immediate danger of the ravages of tsunamis.

A month after the tsunamis, I noticed that Americans were settling down to their old "life as usual" mode of thinking and living. While we cannot live our life in fear and under perpetual uncertainty, I believe that humanity will soon forget the lessons nature tried to convey. I am afraid that we will soon revert to our usual unquenchable hunger for more and more. We will again chase valuables at the expense of our values. We will forsake our kinship with humanity and live as though we were the center of the universe. Things we consider so precious during adversity will soon be taken for granted. Many will begin to mourn, groan, complain, and proclaim that life has dealt them a raw deal. It is my hope that you would quit griping and start enjoying the good life that so many are not fortunate to have. It was amazing to observe that when the tsunamis hit, no material thing was more important than one's life. People realized how little we need to be truly happy. Don't go back to loving valuables over your true values.

In 1963, a dam to the north of the city of Pune, India broke. Much of the city was under ten feet of water. I stood on a hill watching the devastation. I saw a man hanging to a big clay pot in which he had stored all his money. The police threw a rope to the man as he was being swept away and with a megaphone repeatedly warned the man to leave the pot and hang on to the rope. The man chose to hang on the pot and finally drowned.

It is my hope that you would always live and practice the principle of self-renunciation. You must remain the master and not become slave to material things that can be taken away unexpectedly by nature or selfish people.

SOMETHNG TO THINK ABOUT

If you were at sea and your boat was capsized, and there was only one life-jacket, would you offer it to another passenger first?

Do you consider yourself a blessed person? Do you demonstrate your gratitude by being cheerful and by enjoying what you have or do you concentrate on what you do not have?

"Hole in the World"

"There's a hole in the world tonight. There's a Cloud of fear and sorrow.

There's a hole in the world tonight.

Don't let there be a hole in the world tomorrow."

THIS IS ONE of my favorite songs by Eagles. I wish I could quote to you the entire song. It is full of meaning and lessons for real life. I would encourage the reader to go and purchase the album and listen to it, it could change the way you live. I have listened to this song many times. Each time I listen to it, I become acutely aware that I am on this earth for a purpose. I am entrusted with a very unique and very special responsibility to ensure that I leave this earth a little bit better than when I inherited it. With the realization that each one of us plays a key role in ensuring the survival of this planet, we would find purpose for our actions. We would make choices that would be carefully calculated and deliberate. We would examine the impact of each thought, each word, and each action we take. We would look at each encounter with nature, animal kingdom or humans as opportunity to build and enrich what we touch. Each day would bring new possibilities for us to make history and leave our footprints on this earth. Our lives will remind those who come after us that we were not here just for ourselves; we were part of the construction crew on a mission to build this planet as a new and improved place for generations to come. Live with such a purpose in life and make each day meaningful.

From my father I learned that I am a citizen of the universe. This almost gives me a euphoric feeling that transcends social, cultural, language and political boundaries. I don't view people with such backdrops. This earth has had the honor of giving birth to many who have transcended all barriers, and lived to fill the big hole in the world. I think of Mahatma Gandhi, Abraham Lincoln, Mother Teresa, Jesus Christ, Rosa Park, Martin Luther King Jr. I am sure you can add many more to this list. Take time to learn from the lives of these great mentors. They were a gift to humanity. They changed the face of this earth. This earth would never be the same again, and no army on earth can undo the impact they left behind. Reflect on the life and work of these great people and learn how you may fill the big hole in the corner you occupy!

You don't have to be rich or famous in order to fill a big hole in the world. You just have to do your best and make a difference in your little corner of the world – your family, your friendship circle, your church, your community, Little League or just the parent group at your child's school. You don't have to touch the universe to fill a big hole; you just help one person at a time.

SOMETHING TO THINK ABOUT

There is a hole in every heart. Do you feel the hole in your heart? Would you like to fill the hole in your heart? Go touch someone. Become a heart-healer and see the hole in your heart disappear like the dew at sunrise. Let no one slip by you with a hole in his/her heart. In jest, I told my son that I would like the song, "Hole in the World" by Eagles to be played at the conclusion of my funeral. I would like to believe that I will leave a big hole in the world when I depart and that someone would fill it. Am I living a life that would truly result in a big hole in the world when I leave? Would anyone feel it, or would they rather whisper, "Good riddens?" I have become more conscious of my choices. I do want to leave a big hole in the world upon departing. How about you? Will there be someone to fill the big hole we leave behind?

It's Almost Time. Are You Ready?

WHEN I HIT the big 60, my wife wanted to punctuate it with a big fanfare but I restrained her. I became acutely conscious that time was running out for me rapidly. One of these days my family would be unexpectedly plunged into thinking about what to say at my grave site. In the audience would be some who truly feel hurt because I am gone (I hope!), some would be there because they feel bad for my family, some would be there out of obligation, and some would be there just to see if anyone else shows up to bid me goodbye. I sure don't know the exact time of my leaving and that's a blessing. If you are a wise person, not knowing the time of your departure helps you remain ready at all times. Knowing the exact time may make one take it easy and procrastinate preparation. I don't know the time when I may have to bid goodbye to this earth. I remain ready at all times. If I were to go today, I will have no regrets. How about you?

On September 11, 2004, around 7:00 a.m., I went to see a pastor at his church in San Bernardino, California. After a few minutes of conversation, he requested that I return at 7:00 p.m. and speak to his entire congregation about "Life, It's Meaning and Purpose." When I arrived at his church in the evening, the church was empty. There were only three persons walking back and forth and crying. I introduced myself and told them that the pastor had invited me to speak to the congregation. They informed me that at 3:00 p.m. the pastor breathed his last while seated in his rocking chair. I was speechless. Do you suppose he was ready to go?

I believe he was. What if you had to depart this planet suddenly? Are you packed and ready?

I am told that every morning when a policeman kisses his spouse or children to go on duty, he is fully aware that it could be his last kiss, and for many, unfortunately, it is. It pays to remain ready! There is a unique joy in going through the day knowing that the preparation is complete.

I am either getting wiser or paranoid, but in either case, I am realizing that I cannot take life for granted, nor squander it. I must learn to invest it well. Knowing that the end may come abruptly and unexpectedly, I have quit reading good books. I read only the best. I no longer wait for things to happen; I carefully plan my day. I no longer just bump into people; I consciously choose the people I want to touch. I no longer allow circumstances to decide what happens in my business dealings; I keep the end result in mind and make my choices accordingly. If I have money, I don't just go window shopping, I make a list of what I really need and invest wisely. I don't allow my interactions with people to end on a sour note; I make sure that people go feeling better than when they came to see me. I work as though it was my last opportunity to make a difference. I help others as though it was my last chance to touch someone. I live as though it was my last moment but I plan ahead, in case I have the privilege to linger a little longer. How about you? Whether you believe in the Great Spirit or not, I hope that at the end of your road, you will have a smile on your face and you will not be afraid of the big white cloud in the sky!

SOMETHING TO THINK ABOUT

Is your road paved with happy memories of people you blessed? Is your road sprinkled with flowers reminding you of celebration of life? Develop an exit plan and remain ready at all times.

"Bad Moon Rising"

By J. Fogerty

I see a bad moon a rising
I see trouble on the way
I see earthquakes and lightning'
I see bad times today
Don't go around tonight
Well, it's bound to take your life
There's a bad moon on the rise

I hear hurricanes a blowin'
I know the end is comin' soon
I feel river's over-flowin'
I hear the voice of rage and ruin
Don't go around tonight
Well, it's bound to take your life
There's a bad moon on the rise.

Hope you got your things together
Hope you are quite prepared to die

Look like we're in for nasty weather

One eye is taken, for an eye

Don't go around tonight

Well, it's bound to take your life

There's a bad moon on the rise

Don't go around tonight

Well, it bound to take your life

There's a bad moon on the rise.

SOMETHING TO THINK ABOUT

What do you make of the "Bad Moon," hurricane and lightning? Is there any message for this planet? Has this affected your life and work? Have you reordered your priorities?

Give Love a Chance

MEET MR. LOVE and hear his story in his own words. "My name is Love. I was born in the heart of God. However, my ears are ringing by hearing people assert that they can trace my birth to a 'Blind fool who hatched me and let me loose.' My roots go a long ways. Throughout history, I have been saddled with a mix bag of goods. While I have been credited with some notable history-making and life-changing powers, I also have the dubious distinction of bearing the blame for a host of heartbreaking tragedies." Here are just a few of the undesirables that Mr. Love has been blamed for:

Toppling kingdoms;

Creating single moms;

Rudeness and ruthlessness;

Aborted and abandoned children;

All the headaches and heartaches;

Unfaithfulness and secret affairs;

Starting wars and rumors of wars;

Smoked out lives and forest fires;

Broken homes, shattered dreams;

Deceptive plots and broken hearts;

Lack of child support and alimony;

Betrayals of trust and starving children;

Yielding a bumper crop of deadbeat dads;

Messed up priorities and failed businesses;

Creating psychotics, neurotics and lunatics;

Giving people herpes, syphilis, AIDS and death;

Driving people away from their families and God; and

Breaking laws, speeding tickets and incarceration of human soul.

SOMETHING TO THINK ABOUT

"If I had the time and you had the patience, you would hear how I have been blamed for the bad weather, tule-fog, bald-tires, smoked-engines, pot-holes in the road, lack of books in the library and all those who cannot read or write. You would think I would be discouraged; far from it. I still mend lives, rekindle romances, give people hope and make their dreams come true. When the doctors give up and the psychiatrist cannot see you because you have run out of money, call me. I am still alive and well. I make my rounds and I am at work 24/7/365. Give me a chance! You deserve my service. I will go where no one dares to and I will accomplish the unthinkable."

"The Rose"

Some say love, it is a river
that drowns the tender reed.
Some say love, it is a razor
that leaves your soul to bleed.
Some say love, it is a hunger,
an endless aching need.
I say love; it is a flower,
and you its only seed.

It's the heart afraid of breaking
that never learns to dance.
It's the dream afraid of waking
that never takes the chance.
It's the one who won't be taken,

who cannot seem to give,
and the soul afraid of dyin'
that never learns to live.

When the night has been too lonely
and the road has been too long,
and you think that love is only
for the lucky and the strong,
just remember in the winter,
far beneath the bitter snow,
lies the seed that with the sun's love,
in the spring becomes the rose.

As a Man Thinks in His Mind, So is He

A WISE MAN once said, "As a person thinks in his heart, so is he (she)..." The ancient people used the word heart interchangeably with the mind. Heart does not think; it simply pumps the blood to keep the body alive. Thoughts are manufactured in the mind. So watch out where your thoughts may lead you. In your pursuit of "Building a Better You," you must guard your mind and make sure that your thoughts don't take you and abandon you in the land of regrets and remorse.

- As a wheel surely follows the oxen that are pulling the cart, man will certainly follow where his thoughts lead him.

- As a shadow follows a person, man definitely follows his thoughts like a captive follows his master. Are you in control of your thoughts or are they guided by your circumstances?

- By deliberate choice, man travels on the wings of his thoughts, then why is he so surprised at the destination? Where do you think your thoughts are taking you?

- Mind is the factory where all thoughts are hatched. It would be prudent to guard all the gates to your mind to ensure that nothing enters it that would give rise to compromising thoughts. Who is guarding the gates to your mind?

- What we see, hear, speak, touch and smell influences our thought process. These senses are the windows to the portals of our mind. You have heard the "Farmer's Law," "Whatever you sow, that you shall reap." What are you sowing in your mind?

GUARD YOUR MIND & IMPROVE THE QUALITY OF YOUR THOUGHTS

- Train your mind for living well.
- If you cannot fix it, don't meddle.
- Say only what you know to be true.
- Think and listen more. Speak less.
- Read only what will enrich your mind.
- Train your mind for "abundant thinking."
- Touch it if you can heal it or improve it.
- Train your mind for "possibility thinking."
- Train your mind for "pure potential" thinking.
- Be careful on what you leave your finger prints.
- Speak only when it would add value to someone.
- Lend your ear only to the one who can fill it with good news.
- Speak only if it will help build a better relationship and generate peace.
- Use your sense of smell wisely. If it smells like trouble, stay away from it.
- Most people have premonitions. They know when they should stay clear and silent.
- Feed your mind health-enhancing vocabulary: Love, joy, peace, harmony, loyalty, integrity, friendship, faithfulness, truth, kindness, fairness, contentment and steadfastness.

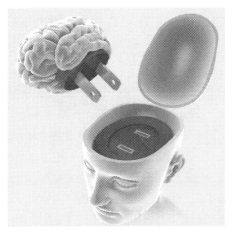

Empty Your Mind of Myths about Excellence

DURING ONE OF my visits to India, I met a person who was overweight and had difficulty in walking. She used a cane to support her weight and maintain balance. I advised her caretaker that if she were to lose her excess weight, she would have no difficulty in walking normally. A year later, I visited the person again. She had lost all the excess weight. I was apprised by her family that when she saw that her legs had lost the excess weight, she felt that her legs were too skinny and weak to support her weight. As a result, she was now bedridden. She would simply lie flat on the bed and refuse to sit or walk. She had created a myth that had grounded her movements. Although she was now physically fit, she was mentally incapacitated. When mind goes out, the body is paralyzed. Heal your mind first!

Many people lock themselves up in imaginary cages and deprive their businesses of their potential. I once saw a huge elephant in India tied to a small stake in the ground with a thin rope. I asked the trainer how such a tiny rope could hold such a powerful animal. "Sir, I have been training this elephant since it was a baby. I have always tied it with the same rope. It still thinks it cannot break the rope or uproot the stake." So it is with people; if at one time, we were unable to do a certain thing, we engrave in our mind that we are not suited for that task. We create myths, believe them and live them as though they were the mandates from God. Here are some myths, that unless you debunk them, they will hold you hostage and paralyze you.

MYTH #1: THINKING THAT WE HAVE ALREADY ARRIVED AT OUR DESTINATION

Bill Shoemaker, the all-time jockey died on October 13, 2003 at the age of 72. He was born on August 23, 1931 as a premature baby. He weighed only two pounds and was not expected to live. He survived, grew up to be 4 feet 11 inches, weighed just 95 pounds and wore size 2 ½ shoes. He broke the world record for winning 8,833 horse races, including four Kentucky Derby races – the only jockey to earn $100 million in his life career. His life story is one of the most remarkable stories. The night before he rode the horse Gallant Man in the 1957 Kentucky Derby, the horse owner Ralph Lowe had told Shoemaker that he had a dream in which one of his riders misjudged the finish line and lost. Shoemaker insisted that it would not happen to him. The next day, Shoemaker stood up on the sixteenth pole mistaking it to be the finish line and lost the race (Taken from Internet 10/13/03).

To run a mile in four minutes was considered to be a pipedream until May 6, 1954 when Roger Bannister set the world record by running a mile in 3.59.4 at Oxford, England. After setting the world record, the 25-year old native of Harrow on the Hill, England, retired, pursued medical studies and became a neurologist. Since then, many have beaten that record, Emil Zatopek and Don Bowden and others.

If your mind can conceive it, your body can deliver it. Your mind sets the limits. When you believe you have reached as far and as high as you can get, the game is over. Its time to call quits. We are created with unlimited potential and we are given powers to keep pushing the envelope until we breathe our last. We must either grow or die. On a journey of life, there is no parking on the dance floor. Unless you remain hungry, no one can feed you. You will eventually starve and die as an irrelevant person of no value to yourself, your family or your company.

MYTH #2: TAKING COMFORT IN THE FACT THAT YOU ARE A COMPANY MAN

American companies are full of good "company men and women." However, in pursuit of excellence, being **good** is not good enough for a company. Being born in a garage does not make one an automobile. Being part of a company does not mean that one is good for the company. Company men and women must also be competent to cxccute their responsibilities. They must add value to the company. They must bring something valuable to the table or they are "good excess baggage." They impede the company's progress. Here are a few questions to ask yourself if you are good for your company?

- If I were to leave my company, will anyone miss what I do?
- If I were to leave my company, will they replace me with someone?
- If I were to leave my company, will there be a negative impact on the company's bottom line or its standing in the community?
- Do I promote unity and harmony of purpose in my company?
- Do I build people around me so they may build the company?

MYTH #3: TAKING COMFORT IN DOING BETTER THAN YOUR COMPETITORS

This is one of the greatest myths of all. Doing better than our competitors is a poor standard to live by. The pursuit of excellence demands DOING OUR BEST, not just doing better than our competitors. Think of two groups contesting for the state championship. Finally, team A wins by scoring 65 out of 100 while their competitor achieved just 62. Would you walk around with your chest swollen because you received a D+ while your competitor received just a D? Get your mind aligned. If you are capable of achieving an A, it would be worthless to gloat over receiving a C because your competitor received a D. Set your own goal high, develop a plan to achieve it, light a fire to work your plan until the goal is reached, and set a new standard of excellence for yourself for the future.

MYTH #4: LIVING ON THE SUCCESS OF THE PAST

I went to school with a man who used to be a wrestler. He lifted weights, jogged his sox off, did all sorts of gymnastics to keep his body fit. However, when he joined the college, he gave up wrestling, quit his physical fitness routine and his muscles began to sag. He gained weight and lost his youthful image. In groups, he would often brag about his past, and almost always, someone would remark, "Have you looked in the mirror lately?" You will never revisit yesterday. An Olympic athlete cannot be given a gold medal again for what he did in 2005. The world will never crown Miss America again for winning the beauty contest in 2005. The world is full of people who "used to be stars." However, unless you are twinkling at the present, you do not shed any light on the future of your family, neighborhood or company.

Living on the accomplishments of the past is like being satisfied having eaten a good meal last week but starving ever since. The past is a good teacher to help us avoid repeating our mistakes. The future is valuable just to remind us that we can start all over and improve our tomorrow. However, neither will fill our stomach today. Shun the myth and get with it. Attend to business at hand as though there is not going to be any tomorrow. Ask yourself the following questions:

- Am I a better contributing member of my family, neighborhood and company than I was last year?

- Am I closer to my goal of achieving happiness than I was a year ago?

- Am I more satisfied with what I am doing to accomplish my life's purpose today than last year?

- Am I a better people builder now than I was two years ago?

MYTH #5: LIVING IN A FANTASY LAND THAT WE CAN DO IT WITHOUT OTHERS

When I worked in the automobile industry, I had a young salesman who had all the ingredients for becoming a superstar but he suffered from the "I am better than all" disorder. One month he sold twenty-three cars. He was far ahead of most of his colleagues in the number of cars sold. He came to my office and began to down his fellow salesmen. He began to boast about his closing skills. I asked him as to how many deals were referred to him by other salesmen. "Thirty-three," he replied. How many were your own customers? "Three," he replied. I looked into his eyes and told him that had the other salesmen not referred to him their deals this month, he would have sold only three cars. I reminded him that without his colleagues, he would have gone home with a very small pay check. You need others to make you a superstar. Be good to people. Love people so they may bless you. The more they like you, the more they are willing to enable you to succeed.

Fools ride on the wings of pride and when they fall, they land in a land of the lonely and poor. Ray Crock, the founder of McDonald's; once said, "I would rather have 1% of 100 people than a 100% of my own efforts." Today you can see what McDonald's has accomplished in the business world. We need one another to achieve our goals.

You need people. In order for a pilot of a plane to have a safe trip, there are dozens of people who work behind the scene to prepare his plane. In order for a space shuttle to have a successful mission, hundreds of scientists spend thousands of hours to work out the details.

I feel sorry for a person who, when given advice, blurts out "I already know." There is no hope for such a person. I feel even more sorrow for a person who thinks he already knows and he does not need anyone's help. Answer these questions:

- How much money would your company make if your boss decided that he did not need any customers?

- How much money would your boss make if he thought he did not need any employees?

- How would a candidate be elected president if he thought he did not need anyone's vote?

Don't bury your head in the sand. We need one another and we were created to help one another.

MYTH #6: LIVING WITH A FALSE BELIEF THAT WHAT YOU KNOW IS ENOUGH

When I was in graduate school, the computer took almost half the room. It is reported that the founder of Microsoft, Bill Gates once said, "Who would want more than 40 GB?" Imagine! What if Bill Gates felt that what he knew about computers in the early 1970's was enough to know! Imagine if the scientists felt that what they knew about space in the 1960's was all there was to know. It is reported that 90% of what we know today was not in existence five years ago. What you know should not shut off your brain, instead, it should serve as the foundation to know more; it should intensify the fire within your heart to learn more. It should make you hungrier to search for more. If your cup is full, no one can bless you by putting something in it. If your mind is full and closed, it will deprive you of what awaits you.

MYTH #7: BELIEVING AND LIVNG AS THOUGH YOU HAVE PLENTY OF TIME

The greatest deception of all is the belief that *WE HAVE PLENTY OF TIME.* If there is a devil, and I believe there is, he has the loudest laugh when he can make people believe that they have plenty of time. The late country music superstar, Tammy Wynette had a song, "I thought I had plenty of time."

Time is like a stallion on a race track. If you are not on it, you are a lap behind and before you know it, the race is over and you have nothing to celebrate.

Live with a sense of urgency. Even the Good Book advises us, "Whatever your hand finds to do, do it with all your might." If the doctor tells you that you have only three more months to live, how would you use the three remaining months of your life? Life is like a bird flying in the air – You have no idea when and where it may end its journey. Time is life and it is more valuable than we realize. Cherish every second and make the best use of it. You will never go back in time where you stood a second ago.

7 Tips to Recharge Your Battery

1. UNPLUG ALL ACCESSORIES: When a car is running, its battery is getting recharged and it can allow us to operate many accessories, i.e. radio, CD/DVD player, cell phone, hearing aide, and even a television. However, when the car is parked, and the battery is not being recharged, if the accessories are not unplugged, the battery will be drained in a short time and the vehicle will be rendered inoperable.

Similarly, the human battery must be recharged or it eventually will bring everything to a screeching halt. For peak performance, the human battery must be recharged by unplugging all accessories that drain our energy. I recommend a thirty minutes' turbo charge in the morning and in the evening. Find a place in the house where no one can disturb you. Sit on the floor with your hands in your lap and your eyes closed. Unplug all distractions – television, radio, cell phone, or any other activity that would disrupt your focus. Turn on the video machine of your mind and recall all the best things that have happened to you. If any negative tape begins to play, immediately turn it off. Stay with the positive experiences you have had – wonderful people you have met, enjoyable job experiences, places you have visited, and things that have made a great positive impact on you.

2. PLUG YOUR MIND INTO THE MINDS OF GREAT PEOPLE: I recommend that you plug into the minds of history-making giants such as – Jesus Christ, Abraham Lincoln, Mahatma Gandhi, Mother Teresa, Nelson Mandela, Martin Luther King Jr. and Albert Schweitzer. You may have other great mentors who have impacted you positively. Read about their life experiences and what motivated them to take the road they took.

3. REALIGN YOUR MIND AND YOUR LIFE PRIORITIES: Take a purposeful walk through the garden of your mind and assess your ways of thinking, believing and behaving. Eliminate the negative elements. Mend or end what distracts and drains your motivation to excel. Replace what you discard with noble ideas and innovative thoughts you picked by plugging into the minds of great people.

4. DEVELOP AN ATTITUDE OF GRATITUDE: Do you realize that you are the most fortunate person on the face of the earth? Consider this: Nearly 75% of the world's population has less than two pairs of clothes. How many do you have? More than 75% of the world's population has unsafe drinking water. Do you ever worry about the water you drink? There are millions who have lost an arm, a hand, a leg or some part of the body, millions are unable to see, hear or speak, millions are confined to a bed in a convalescent hospital, millions are waiting for an organ transplant, hundreds of millions have lost their homes and jobs, and are worried about where the next meal will come from. If you are breathing, you are more fortunate than the millions who breathed their last this morning. So develop an attitude or gratitude and your battery will have a turbo charge.

5. ADOPT A CAUSE GREATER THAN YOURSELF: When we reach out and touch a soul in need and be the solution that fits that moment, we become God-incarnate for that soul. To that man or a woman, we become God-in-flesh, walking, talking and serving people where they are. To a person in need, we become the heaven-sent angels of good news.

6. BALANCE YOUR LIFE: Know the difference between your wants and your needs. Meet your needs first. Live on a budget. Always spend less than you make. Set aside at least enough money to live on for six months in case hard times invade your household. Ensure equal development of all aspect of your life – Your personal wellness, family life, spiritual health, business and social life. Have 7-8 hours of sleep, 7-8 glasses of water daily, regular breakfast, good lunch and a light supper, a minimum of 30 minutes of walk daily, refrain from tobacco, caffeine, and alcohol. Finally, maintain ideal weight and minimize your stress by reducing stress for others who live and work with you.

7. TAKE TIME TO PLAY AND CELEBRATE: Set aside some time each day or each week to have fun. We were not created to be a non-stop working machine. We were created to have a good time and celebrate life. So make time for fun. Read a good book, watch a healthy movie, go for skiing, hiking, walking in the park, working in the garden, playing with your children, visiting friends, the elderly and the poor. Make time for playing with your spouse, getting a massage, and volunteering to make this world a better place than when you first found it.

Celebrate and honor those who smiled at you, those who opened the door for you, those who encouraged you when chips were down, and those who shook your hand to let you know they support you.

When I jump start the life of someone whose battery is dead, my life's battery receives a turbo charge. If I can put a smile on the face of the one who has no way to reciprocate, my battery is fully recharged and my life is running on all 16 cylinders. So go and recharge your battery and live your life to your fullpotential.

Travel Safely – Don't Believe Myths

LET TRUTH AND reality be the bricks and mortar of your character building - the dream mansion you have been constructing since you were born. Those who substitute myths and wishful thinking in the place of truth and reality, are building castles in the sand. Departure from truth and reality gives birth to pipe dreams that last as long as the bubbles on the water. People who defy reality ultimately drown themselves in the sea of disappointments. Let me introduce you to some familiar myths that you will encounter on your journey of life.

Myths and Realities

Myth: The world owes you something.

Reality: Get a life! This fat world owes you nothing.

Myth: Your body will be good to you even if you abuse it.

Reality: There will be a day of judgment; garbage in, garbage out!

Myth: That you can live happily while spending beyond your means.

Reality: It's time to wake up. You are burying your head in the sand.

Myth: That you must be appreciated when you do something good.

Reality: Get ready to be kicked in the shin, criticized and ignored.

Myth: You have the right to celebrate without making a sacrifice.

Reality: Not so! Every dream has a price, and if realized, a prize.

Myth: No one will ever find out what you think or do in secret.

Reality: That's a deception. Walls have ears. It all comes out.

Myth: All your plans will come to pass just as you expected.

Reality: It's a pipedream. Be realistic, and don't fall apart.

Myth: Someone out there is looking out for your success.

Reality: Get a life! If it's going to be, it's up to you.

Myth: The more money you make, the happier you'll be.

Reality: After basic needs are met, money brings woes.

Myth: It could not be wrong if everyone else is doing it.

Reality: The majority is rarely right. Don't follow the crowd.

Myth: I too would be successful if I were born with a silver spoon.

Reality: Many of the rich and famous were born in abject poverty.

(Oprah Winfrey, Abraham Lincoln, Nelson Mandela, Mother Teresa, Gandhi).

Myth: I am too old. It's too late for me to make a new start in life.

Reality: As long as there is life, there is hope. Don't be a quitter.

Myth: You don't have to be nice to people who push you around.

Reality: Being nice is not optional, if you are building a better you!

Myth: Belief that someone or something can make you happy.

Reality: Happiness is the result of a choice, not a chance.

Myth: You can change how others believe and behave.

Reality: Don't dream of it! You will die a failure.

SOMETHING TO THINK ABOUT

In building a better you, you will often find yourself
on a lonely road, keep trucking to the better end.

Get the
Right Map

HAVE YOU EVER been on a trip in a strange country, looking for your dream resort but you don't know how to get there? Have you ever driven in circles trying to find your destination? Have you ever been lost and frustrated, wishing you had a map to guide you? Have you ever traveled with a group of people who thought they knew where they were going, but they led you to a jungle instead, where every trail seemed to lead you to the right place, but the end was disappointing? Have you ever been on a journey with some friends who have all the maps of the world, except the one that would lead you to your desired destination?

No road is more unfamiliar than the road for your journey of life. Although we are not born with a road atlas in our hands, we can acquire the right road map, if we only choose. On your journey of life, you will meet people who are totally lost. They don't have a clue where they are supposed to land in life. Then there are those who keep spinning their wheels but are too proud to ask for directions. The world has no dearth of those who think they know the way. They are traveling at maximum speed, burning rubber, but they wind up at dead end roads that lead only to regrets and disappointments. Some people are just like the hiker who has slipped and fell off the trail 1000 feet below, but refuses to be rescued. You will also meet many who are too smart for their own good. They are like a traveler whose destination is New York but he is loaded with maps of every city in the world, except the map of New York. Where do you think he will end up?

Having irrelevant maps is like having our head full of irrelevant information. It may be good for mental gymnastics, but it is unrelated to our personal, family or company goals. I once had a colleague who was like a walking encyclopedia of irrelevant information. He would walk around the company asking people questions about obscure facts from the past, share information about ancient philosophies, rituals and traditions, while his performance remained marginal at best. He was an intelligent man with a great potential. He reminded me of a jet, loaded with fuel but parked on the runway of life.

Let me paraphrase the advice from the world's all-time best counselor, "Whatsoever your hand finds to do, do it with all your might, because where you are going, there is no more activity." Many years ago, my father shared with me a saying, "Wherever you are, be there." It means to acquire the information and skills to give our best to the people and tasks at hand. It means to weed out irrelevant information and priorities that distract us from the journey to our intended goal. Don't waste your energy on irrelevant and unproductive arguments. Choose your words so your thoughts would lead to purposeful and desired destinations.

In this book, I have attempted to highlight a few guideposts along life's highway. However, many will read these principles of life, file them away, and go about business as usual. I urge you to take an inventory of your life. Make a list of what has been beneficial to you on your journey thus far and do more of that. Identify things that have held you back and bid goodbye to such beliefs and behaviors. Having learned from your past experiences, you are now smarter than you were when you first started your journey. Follow the right map that would lead you to your dream destination. Remember, there is nothing you cannot do. Nothing and no one can hold you back, unless you allow it. Happy journey!

SOMETHING TO THINK ABOUT

Examine the maps in your head and determine if they would lead you to your destination.

My Final Thoughts

NOW THAT YOU have realigned your mind and embarked on a journey to Build a Better You, I hope:

...that you will be happy just being alive;

...that you will laugh your heart out at celebrations;

...that you will never expect something for nothing;

...that you will not expect praise when you do good;

...that you will not ignore when others do a good job;

...that you will leave every place better than you found it;

...that you will congratulate your adversary when he wins;

...that you will never be so poor that you resort to stealing;

...that you will respect the elderly and learn from children;

...that you will shed a few tears with the lonely and grieving;

...that you will never be so rich that you forget your Maker;

...that you will find more happiness in giving than receiving;

...that you will never try to impress others with what you have;

...that you will be grateful for just having a dry toast with water;

...that you will not look down on yourself when you are rejected;

...that you will practice silence when you are tempted to criticize;

...that you will lose your hunger for controlling people and events;

...that you will always remain a student of life and learn to live well;

…that you will lose your appetite for seeking credit for what you do;

…that you will feed your soul more regularly than stuffing your belly;

…that you will not wait to fill your own barn before you help the poor;

…that you will have a song in your heart with just a shirt on your back;

…that you will not cheat yourself by doing less than you are capable of;

…that you will not tear down your soul while building your bank balance;

…that you will not wait for a heart attack before taking care of your body;

…that you will learn humility by falling and have the courage to start over;

…that you will put a much higher value on relationships than business deals.

…that you will not be ashamed to say you are sorry when you hurt someone;

…that you will always put others first regardless of their economic condition;

…that you will begin building a better world by taking time to improve yourself;

…that you will not expect to be paid more before you do more than you are paid;

…that you will be content having just one true friend than a 1000 phony admirers;

…that you will not be so proud to make a U-turn when wrong, regardless of the investment.

SOMETHING TO THINK ABOUT

What do you think of the statement, "We will never have enough of what we don't need to make us happy?" What can you learn from this statement in your pursuit of "Building a Better You?"

Get your priorities in order and make a commitment to live by your priorities and make the rest of your life memorable. Buy the album "My Next Thirty Years," by Tim McGraw and live the message. It would bring a new meaning to your life and a purpose to your actions.

"My Next Thirty Years"

Written by Phillip Vassar, Performed by Tim McGraw

I think I'll take a moment to celebrate my age
The ending of an era and the turning of a page
Now it's time to focus in on where I go from here
Lord, have mercy on my next thirty years

Hey, my next thirty years, I'm gonna have some fun
Try to forget about all the crazy things I've done
Maybe now I've conquered all my adolescent fears
And I'll do it better in my next thirty years

My next thirty years, I'm gonna settle all the scores
Cry a little less, laugh a little more
Find a world of happiness without the hate and fear
Figure out just what I'm doing here in my next thirty years

Oh, my next thirty years, I'm gonna watch my weight
Eat a few more salads and not stay up so late
Drink a little lemonade and not so many beers
Maybe I'll remember my next thirty years

My next thirty hears will be the best years of my life
Raise a little family and hang out with my wife
Spend precious moments with the ones that I hold dear
Make up for lost time here in my next thirty years
In my next thirty years.

It is better to live just forty days with a purpose than to wander in the wilderness aimlessly for forty years!